Atoms, Snowflakes & God

QUEST BOOKS
are published by
The Theosophical Society in America,
a branch of a world organization
dedicated to the promotion of brotherhood and
the encouragement of the study of religion,
philosophy, and science, to the end that man may
better understand himself and his place in
the universe. The Society stands for complete
freedom of individual search and belief.
In the Theosophical Classics Series
well-known occult works are made
available in popular editions.

Cover design by *Jane A. Evans*

Atoms, Snowflakes & God

The Convergence of Science and Religion

By JOHN L. HITCHCOCK

This publication made possible with the assistance of the Kern Foundation

The Theosophical Publishing House
Wheaton, Ill. U.S.A.
Madras, India/London, England

©Copyright John L. Hitchcock, 1982.
A Quest original. First edition, 1986.

The Theosophical Publishing House
306 West Geneva Road
Wheaton, Illinois 60189

A publication of the Theosophical Publishing House, a department of the Theosophical Society in America.

Library of Congress Cataloging in Publication data.

Hitchcock, John L., 1936-
  Atoms, snowflakes & God

  (A Quest book)
  Based on the author's dissertation.
  Bibliography: p.
  Includes index.
  1. Religion and science, 1946-   . I. Title. II. Title:
Atoms, snowflakes, and God.
BL240.2.H528 1986 215 85-40842
ISBN 0-8356-0604-X (pbk.)

Printed in the United States of America.

Dedication

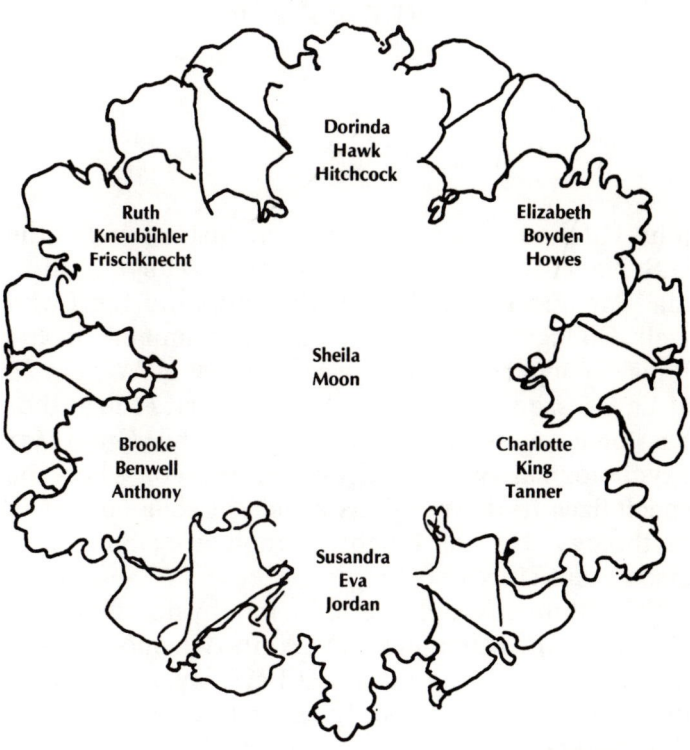

Dorinda
Hawk
Hitchcock

Ruth
Kneubühler
Frischknecht

Elizabeth
Boyden
Howes

Sheila
Moon

Brooke
Benwell
Anthony

Charlotte
King
Tanner

Susandra
Eva
Jordan

About the Author

John Hitchcock has taught physics/astronomy at the U.S. Naval Nuclear Power School at Vallejo, California, San Francisco State University, and the Cogswell College and is presently a member of the Physics Department at the University of Wisconsin at La Crosse. In addition, for many years the author has been a seminar leader with the Guild for Psychological Studies of San Francisco, where he specializes in the religious aspect of science and in mythology. He has taught mythology at San Francisco State University.

Dr. Hitchcock holds a B.S. in Physics from the University of Michigan, a M.A. in Astronomy from the University of California at Berkeley, and a Ph.D. in the Phenomenology of Science and Religion from the Graduate Theological Union at Berkeley.

Contents

Preface   ix

Introduction   1

1 Consciousness   11
    Consciousness, Spirit, and Matter
    The Relatedness of Opposites
    The Stuff of the Universe
    God in Human Knowledge
    The Value of Separateness

2 Reality, Being, Existence   29
    Reality
    Physical Reality
    Spiritual Reality
    Being and Existence
    Phenomenological Grounding
      for Reality
    The Ego and Levels of Reality

3 The Way of Knowing   63
    Spirit, Matter, and Ego Consciousness

4 Complementarity   94
    In Physics
    Of Ego and Unconscious
    A Symbol of the Complementarity
      Relationship

5 Spirit-Matter   118
    Small Whole Numbers and Reality
    Spirit as Patterning in Evolution

6 Holographic Evolution   151
    Love
    Freedom
    Consciousness
    Meaning

Appendix A - Particles and Waves   191

Appendix B - The Uncertainty Principle   195

Appendix C - Kierkegaard on the
           Concept of Time   197

References   199

Index   205

Preface

Years ago as a physics undergraduate, I encountered some attitudes that challenged me. I call these negative attitudes "ultrarationalism" and "nothing but." They are the standard stock of the intellectual "put-down artists," and work together to form a rather easy-to-defend system. Within their outlook all that is nonrational is simply forbidden, as well as all that is spiritual. Many with a natural tendency to take refuge in this outlook gravitate to mathematics and the hard physical sciences, or did in those days.

I encountered the rationalistic turn of mind in teachers who told me that the question as to whether the true nature of light is wave or particle is meaningless, implying that such questions don't have a rationalistic answer. This struck a contradictory note within me. I knew that, historically speaking, many such questions have become the nuclei of profound changes in cultural ideas. To me the lack of a rationalistic answer more often than not signals a deep question and the presence of something further to be discovered.

The "nothing but" mentality believes in nothing but what can be immediately touched or measured. In particular, much in the line of spiritual phenomena is labeled illusory without investigation, because it is impossible. My response to this has been an attempt to account for the religious ideas that have gripped individuals and cultures, evoking great art and philosophical depth and imbuing individuals with tremendous spirit and courage. The fact that persons are willing to die for the sake of an ideal indicates that there is *in fact* something spiritual to be accounted for.

To challenge these negative attitudes from within the sciences is to make one's own path difficult, but without adequate training in the sciences it is impossible. The task is, then, to discover whatever is *real* that the rationalists are excluding and to gather evidence that it *is* real. My two concerns—for solid evidence and for the inclusion of all that is factual— came together in my endeavor. While I continually deal with the symbolic level, which Teilhard de Chardin called "the *within* of things," and which through evolution has become our own inwardness, my deep concern is that all I present is good physics. This concern is by no means limited to what is present *as* physics, for some aspect of physics is implied in every philosophical and religious concern as well.

All of this might well have remained a very personal journey, and I might have felt no particular need to communicate what I had discovered, both on my own and from those whose works this need of mine drove me to read. Indeed, I was on such an introverted path when I discovered that I actually was becoming what I had assimilated. When someone was interested in *who* I am, I had to try to say something about this search into which I had invested so much energy. Then came the discovery, remarkable to me, that this material held interest for others. In fact, I was not nearly so alone as I had thought. Not only were my friends interested, but books were being written in precisely this area. Of course, it should have been more evident to me that I was part of the spirit of the times. However, my relative isolation has blessed me with an approach that seems different in a central respect, which needs to be mentioned.

As far as I can see, most other books dealing with comparisons of science and religion come from authors whose desire is to focus on *one* of the world's existing religions. Each of these religions has made a tremendous contribution to that sizeable portion of humanity born into the area of its influence. But their diversity is hardly to be reconciled as these religions now stand. My own point of view is that as we have evolved and continue to evolve, so our religions will continue to evolve and change. Therefore, the question is: Is it possible to find a basis for coming together as humans to a *new* center of focus? If so, won't it be found in some area which is already transcultural, as science is? If all philosophies and religions imply some view of physical reality, the converse may also hold: that physical science implies spirituality in some way. That, at least, is the thrust of this effort. This book is what I can present so far as to the results of my search, results that have also woven themselves together into new classes taught and a doctoral dissertation. I hope that my offering holds value for the stage of development in which we find ourselves.

Through the offices of the Guild for Psychological Studies of San Francisco, several persons unknown to me provided financial support, part of which was designated for the writing of some of this book. I would like to thank the Guild, and those who contributed.

This work is an outgrowth of my dissertation,

though very different from it. Those who contributed to various stages of my progress in the direction I have taken were acknowledged there. Seven women who stand at the very roots of the book, each in her own way, are honored in the snowflake pattern of the dedication.

The students in my Science and Humanities course at San Francisco State University enriched my perspective immeasurably, as did many of my students in introductory astronomy, sharing with me resources from many fields of study, as well as their irreplaceable, enthusiastic selves.

The opportunity to present some of the material of Chapter Five was afforded by the Guild for Psychological Studies on numerous occasions, through its seminars. For this opportunity, which greatly influenced what has been written, I again express thanks to the Guild, but especially to Dr. Elizabeth Boyden Howes, whose encouragement of my work has greatly helped me overcome doubts about my ability to give it the form it deserves.

I am tremendously indebted to Dr. Sheila Moon for the title of the book, and for many hours of consultation in the development of its contents. The diagram of the "Present State of the Cosmos" in Chapter Three owes much to her. She read most of the chapters in preliminary form, and she examined some sections as a member of my doctoral committee. Dr. Glenn Bacon, Dr. Walter Wink, The Reverend Judith Gray Anders-Richards, and Ruth Frischknecht read the entire book in semifinal form and gave numerous pages of valuable comments. Anne Ogonowski typed the manuscript. Her generosity with time and her concern for the project of the publication of the first small printing, have indeed brought it to this point of real birth.

Dorinda, my wife, read portions of the book onto a tape for a friend, and her perceptions enabled me to smooth out places which otherwise would not have been noticed. Dorinda's practical, daily, religious use of this material has not only been a deep inspiration to me but has become a continuing source of rich insights for both of us, many of which have found their way into the text. For unfailing support in uncertain years, for laughter, and for so much more, I can't hope to say how grateful I am.

Introduction

Science and religion are two ways of knowing reality. We all have a general sense of the difference of these two paths, such as that science focuses upon matter and religion upon spirit or spirituality. Both fields have their phenomena, methods, and attitudes. Science deals with precisely reproducible conditions in order to limit the possible causes which may be producing a phenomenon, and thus distinguishes between competing theories of the structure of matter. It attempts to be completely objective so that its results are independent of which scientist does an experiment. Religion is harder to define because there is less general agreement as to what it is among those who practice its various forms. It is, however, seen as more on the subjective side, and religious experience for the participant is one of its goals.

On closer examination, neither of these divisions holds absolutely. Religion finds itself involved with matter and science with spirit. The process of scientific creativity has often involved inspiration and mythic elements, as shown by philosophers of science such as Thomas Kuhn in *The Structure of Scientific Revolution* (1970), Gerald Holton in *Thematic Origins of Scientific Thought* (1973), and by others as well. The question of whether we observe the thing-in-itself or whether we "filter" the perceptions, seeing only what we are adapted to see, has been open since Kant and has been the field of much discussion, some of which will be found in this book. In the case of religion, the noted theologian Paul Tillich has been a spokesperson for its objective or philosophical side. In his *Biblical Religion and the Search for Ultimate Reality* (1964), he presents this side both in opposition to and in unity with the subjective side of religious experience.

Because the rigid separation of these and other pairs of classical oppositions between science and religion have broken down, we are compelled to consider the possibility of the mutual dependence of these two ways, or even the convergence of science and religion as ultimately similar, even in their aims and methods.

For this purpose, it is necessary to give a more general view of religion than is usually held. In this book religion is to be seen in its ultimate etymological sense as "binding back together," relinking. A ligament is a link which holds two things together. The word element *re* implies that what is to be held or bound together was once together and has come apart. It can be simply stated that what has come apart are human consciousness and its ground, the unconscious. Consciousness and the unconscious are what need reintegration and that, in numerous forms, is religion.

Many thought systems which profess to be nonreligions can be seen as religious in this sense. For example, Buddhism claims not to be a religion, but when a Zen master asks the disciple to "show me your original face" (a famous problem or "koan"), he or she is calling for reconnection, that is, religion in the sense just given.

Religion, again in the sense used here, has nothing

to do with the assumption or assertion of an existing God. However, if our examination of evolution shows that something purposive is at work in that process and in our lives now, perhaps *God* is a good word for that perceived purposive reality. This has nothing to do with belief. It is rather a matter of evidence and knowledge, or at least the interpretation of known facts.

It should be clear from the title of this book that I feel the evidence to be given is sufficient to employ the word *God* but I have no wish to force this view onto others. I am moved always to present facts. To me they have rejuvenated the word *God*, and I am glad to share this experience with others.

In the case of science, we will need to broaden the view of what it is since it too has its "sectarian" divisions, favoring various "standard" approaches to experimentation or theorization.

In order to contemplate the convergence of science and religion on the broadest possible basis, it will be necessary to assume that no one's cherished position will necessarily be vindicated. In the realm of religion, for example, we must not assume that the results will favor Christianity, Buddhism, Hinduism, Judaism, Taoism, or any other particular religious way. In science we must not assume a favoring of any given mathematical formalism, or even of certain logical or rational rules.

At the same time we must have some recourse, some way of grounding our thoughts and of expressing facts and theories. For this difficult process, no ultimate rules can be given. We can only begin where we are, proceed carefully, and attempt to avoid unconscious preconceptions. Roots of our conscious preconceptions must be given. We trust that they will be the best with which to begin.

The primary concern of this book is the continuing

development of human consciousness, but consciousness is difficult to describe because the word is used in many ways. In the case of life in general, we see a continuum of development of degrees of consciousness which points backward in time to ever simpler life forms. But even in the simplest forms we see the rudiments of the development of inwardness or conscious awareness that characterizes the higher life forms. As will be seen, I feel that we can trace the basis of consciousness back even to the primordial atoms themselves. The Jesuit paleontologist, Pierre Tielhard de Chardin, called this capacity for a developed inwardness "the within of things."

Regarding human consciousness, we are able to distinguish different levels of consciousness both within and among ourselves. Within ourselves we distinguish waking and sleeping at the least, and it is clear that some among us can truly be called more conscious than others. Thus, we who are, as far as we can generally determine, the possessors of the most complex minds, and the greatest degree of consciousness when it is fully employed, are also largely unconscious. Moreover, we can anticipate further developments in humanity and in other species with respect to which we can and should be called unconscious, even when we are at our best.

This finite but growing kind of consciousness, which was the concern of the great psychologist C.G. Jung, is always very specific and has a specific individual human carrier. It is concentrated and point-like rather than a diffuse awareness or striving. Following Jung, I will call it "ego-consciousness." This is the kind of consciousness which is undergoing development in evolution. It is both the achievement of the cosmos up to its present level and the goal of continuing evolution. That is, it is partially, but not fully, achieved, and may never be completed.

If consciousness is in the process of development, then, we may ask by what agency. Is it pre-existing mind? I feel their attribution goes beyond the available facts. Biologist Erich Jantsch takes another approach by attributing the agency of evolution to the cosmos itself, as shown in the very title of his book, *The Self-Organizing Universe*. He calls it "an unfolding of order," leading to "self-transcendence" (1980, p. 307). I take a middle ground, feeling that there are factual ways in which we can point to a Patterning behind the innumerable visible patterns. The reason for my use of the capital in Patterning will become clear later.

It is often destructive of definitions to speak, say, of what a hydrogen atom "knows," but certainly the atom possesses many patterns of existence, and it continually employs these and no others. Things develop in a patterned way, and I believe we can also assert that they develop in a *purposeful* way. For this quality, the word *omniscience* seems to serve particularly well. As will be seen in Chapter Six, I attribute *omniscience* to the Patterning, but not consciousness in the sense of ego-consciousness. Only complex organic forms can be conscious (or unconscious) in the Jungian sense.

With this as background on consciousness, it is important to note that one guiding fact underlies the whole development of this book: human consciousness has evolved out of that which is unconscious. The phrase "that which is unconscious" is used instead of "the unconscious" because the latter term usually refers to *human* unconsciousness, the nature of which is quite unlike mineral substances or raw chemical elements. In the present context that which is "unconscious" means primordial matter, which is generally conceded to be pure hydrogen, or more specifically the primal plasma of protons and electrons produced from pure energy (photons) in the Big Bang. We know that this primordial matter is not sufficiently complex to be conscious in the sense that we are conscious. Ego-consciousness seems to require a complex animal organism for its realization. Our guiding fact has wide-ranging implications and, in the largest sense, the contents of this book consist of nothing but implications of this fact.

One of the immediate implications is that the formal opposites, conscious and unconscious, are *related*. This is an apparent contradiction whose nature, along with the nature of the relationship of all such opposites, must be understood in order to assimilate the contents of this book.

The words *conscious* and *unconscious* are *formal* opposites, by which is meant merely the obvious fact that the word element un- is a form by which negation is expressed. The one is the logical negation of the other, but such a statement is far from deep enough to satisfy us. Questions remain, such as: (1) Yes, the words are opposites, but do they really refer to exact opposites in their accepted meanings? (2) What are the exact definitions of each as used in the present context? (3) Are the meanings as employed artificially selected from a range of meanings, some of which remain hidden? (4) Are the concepts fully and totally opposed? (One uses such redundant language for emphasis!) Behind such questions is the desire to be certain of the *separation* of the concepts, in spite of the fact that they are related through the central word *conscious*. If concepts cannot be separated, then all definition becomes fuzzy. But here it is important to notice that the same relatedness is true of *any* formal negation: A and not-A (where A stands for any quality) have A in common. This, though, is a logical kind of relatedness, rather than a factual one.

Our guiding fact makes a different *kind* of statement about the relationship of that which is conscious to that which is unconscious, namely that the one has evolved out of the other. This is a physical statement about the nature of that which exists. It emphasizes the *continuity* between that which is unconscious and that which is conscious, and thus it denies the separation. This seems to be quite a common role of physical facts, to deny rational separatisms which would otherwise seem to us rather obviously to be necessary. We are quite prejudiced in favor of the rational.

Nevertheless this evolution *is* a fact, to the best of our knowledge, and whatever rational process would seem to deny it must therefore give way. At the same time, as will be made clear, rationality is valued equally with fact. It is not, however, given the automatic priority over fact which it has enjoyed in philosophical and scientific circles since Descartes. Rationality plays an indispensible part in a process which amounts to the continual reconciliation between itself and fact. The loss of either would lead to total one-sidedness.

However, since we are less accustomed to accepting cases of the priority of fact over rationality, an example of the use of a nonrational guiding fact may be helpful.

In 1913 Niels Bohr presented a model of the atom in which the idea of electrons circling in orbits around the nucleus of the atom was first given, for which he received the Nobel prize in physics. By assuming that an electron could "jump" from one allowable orbit to another, Bohr was able to explain why hydrogen gives off certain very specific colors of light when electricity is passed through it. Here was a case of a theoretical "model" which could explain observed facts. His model was thus a great triumph, but there were grave difficulties with the idea that an electron could travel in an orbit at all. It was known that an electron traveling in a bent path must experience a loss of energy and that the loss of its energy of motion, by which it stays in orbit, would mean that the electron would very quickly spiral down to the nucleus and could not stay in orbit. Therefore Bohr's model was self-contradictory. But it also explained the stability of matter, the fact that solids have structural strength, which Bohr considered "a pure miracle when considered from the standpoint of classical physics" (quoted from conversation in Heisenberg 1971, p. 39). In addition, it provided an explanation of why physical properties persevere. If classical, rational physics could not explain these simple facts, it should be clear that we must hold to Bohr's model, for matter *is* stable. These facts require that we build a theory upon contradiction. In his famous *Lectures on Physics* (1963, p. 2-6), Feynman expresses it simply:

> So we now understand why we do not fall through the floor... The resistance to atomic compression is a quantum mechanical effect and not a classical effect.

How could it be put more graphically? If we trust the floor, we must somehow learn to trust the contradictoriness of the nature of reality.

Among the manifestations of the contradiction is the famous "uncertainty principle" which will be considered later and the various objections to it answered. Some say that the contradiction is not in the phenomenon itself (a term to be defined), but rather in the nature of human consciousness. This question, too, will be considered.

It is hoped that the foregoing is sufficient to prepare the reader to encounter the viewpoint which will be found in this book. To summarize: this is a study on the necessity of contradiction. It provides a general model for comprehension of the unity of conflicting views and qualities. It is based on a single guiding fact, namely the emergence of that which is conscious out of that which is unconscious. It is phenomenologically grounded in modern physics and substantiated in Kierkegaardian existentalism. It holds implication for psychology, theology, philosophy, science, and, more centrally, for the life of the "existing individual."

The reader will notice that this book is full of references to the writings of C.G. Jung. This is so far from coincidence that I would be very pleased to have the work referred to as a Jungian book. Jung's elucidation of the fact that all our knowledge is psychic by nature and is therefore not direct knowledge of things-in-themselves has been the lever by means of which many problems of physics and philosophy have been raised out of confusion. In particular it has made clear the role of the "observer" in physics. This clarity is a close runner-up on importance to the guiding fact itself. Then comes Jung's work on the nonrationality of the bases of consciousness, the "archetypes," and even their nonperceivability.

Impossible to rank at all, because of the centrality of *meaning* for all human life, is Jung's study of the "God-image" which is part of the psychic reality and organism of all humanity, collective and individual. This God-image, which he called the "Self," with its numinosity and its power both to integrate our lives and to differentiate our intellects, can be seen as a central guiding force in the whole evolution of consciousness out of that which is unconscious. Some of the material in this book is philosophical, psychological, or physical groundwork for the world view which emerges. Because this material naturally comes prior to the conclusions, it has been placed in the early chapters. The conclusions may be found in Chapters Five and Six, but I would encourage the reader to read Chapter One; Chapter Two, pages 29-31 and 39-43, Chapter Three, pages 84-93, and Chapter Four, pages 94-96 before going on to the last two chapters. Even those who are interested in argumentation as such may want to read the pages just listed before going through the first four chapters in detail.

This book is necessarily a mere sketch of a cosmic overview of reality, but I hope I have been reasonably complete and yet have maintained continuity.

1

Consciousness

Knowledge known to none is no knowledge.
Erhard Scheibe, The Logical
Analysis of Quantum Mechanics

We begin in the middle because we *are* in the middle. This point of departure is different from that of philosophy, mathematics, physics, and traditional theology, all of which are forever attempting to establish foundations for their studies. They want to begin from the beginning, but their foundations are always shifting and changing. Beginnings are very elusive. Philosophy, physics, mathematics, and theology have never really established their beginnings. Even our physical cosmos, which seems so definitely to have begun in a great explosion, the Big Bang, some fifteen billion years ago, must be based upon some prior physical existence, although we can't go into that here. The point is that all attempts to establish definitive and universally satisfying beginnings for these fields of study have failed. Therefore, we must take another approach, one which accepts the human condition.

We begin in the middle because we *are* in the middle. We, that is humans, are always "in between," separated from our beginnings and endings, from our ground and potentials; separated from so-called inanimate matter by our relative consciousness, and from superanimate spirit perhaps by our relative unconsciousness. Yet we nonetheless belong to all these things and somehow to each other as well: to earth, to something beyond which in common usage we call God, and to others who share with us the condition of separation. The separation is real, and the belonging or inclusion is real: we *stand* in disrelation and relation. To the separations and belongings already mentioned—God, matter, spirit, other humans—we may add another, namely, ourselves. We are separated from our own wholeness, while belonging to it. But perhaps we are most fully ourselves when we are as fully as possible related to matter, spirit, other humans, and God.

Later, we will look at the whole evolution of the cosmos to see how our condition of separateness but belonging, our in-between-ness, came about, but first I must say a few words about the *value* of the separation to prepare the ground for the convergence of religion and science. Both religion and science are *ways of knowing* about the nature of reality. But to know something requires first that we be separate from it. To know something without being separate from it is to *identify* with it, rather than to be *conscious* of it. Because we are separate subjects, we can stand apart, can distance ourselves from things. Then they are objective to us; we can see that they are beyond our will. Again, only by having become separate can we establish a *relationship* to an objective world of matter, spirit, other humans, and God.

We are concentrating on the relationship called knowing and on religion and science as ways of *knowing*. In both cases our knowledge is *imperfect* because of the separation. But our knowledge of reality can be *whole*, as distinct from perfect, if within ourselves we are able to bring together both religion and science, to establish the relationship between them, and to see *why* a description of reality can never be complete without both.

The relation between religion and science may be explained, in part, in terms of the nature of our *consciousness* and the ways in which *we* know things. That is, it seems to be part of the *human* condition to have two ways of knowing. But also, in part we may see actual objective similarities in science and religion and in the objects which they study. These similarities are there because of an inherent relationship of matter and spirit. To start with, I am taking matter as the object of scientific knowledge and spirit as the object of religious knowledge. If a definite relationship of matter and spirit can be shown, then the relationship of science and religion will become apparent.

CONSCIOUSNESS, SPIRIT, AND MATTER

Consciousness *stands between* matter and spirit. I find that most philosophers have rather *identified* consciousness with the spirit side of our nature. I, on the other hand, feel that we are just as separate from spirit as a thing-in-itself as we are from matter.

Everything which reaches us as knowledge of either spirit or matter has been mediated or transformed in some way so as to become compatible with consciousness. Perhaps some of its unlikeness has been stripped away or filtered out, and perhaps it has been squeezed into a form of likeness which distorts its objective reality into something we can perceive, so that our knowledge of spirit and matter *may* be more knowledge of ourselves than of spirit and matter. Whether one or all of these possibilities is the case is a question which has been studied by physicists, philosophers, and theologians, and it is too involved to go into here. The difference which I see between their position and mine, though, is that I include the nature of spirit-as-such in the unknown, along with the nature of matter-as-such. I find that most others have subtly identified spirit with consciousness. For example, Swiss psychologist Marie-Louise von Franz, in *Number and Time* (1974), expresses a fundamental polarity as that of psyche and matter, whereas I feel that the polarity is spirit and matter with psyche in between. We have *images* of matter but matter-in-itself is unknown to us. Similarly, we have images of spirit, but spirit-in-itself is unknown to us. If it were not so, there would be no shifting of the foundations or no elusiveness of the beginnings. Because it is *not* possible to establish foundations for sciences, we must conclude that something of both matter and spirit *remains* unknown.

To say, then, that consciousness has evolved out of that which is unconscious is to say that consciousness partakes of both spirit and matter and yet is to some degree separate from both.

We experience spirit and matter as distinct aspects of reality, and it appears that no two sets of qualities could be more unlike. To touch an object physically is vastly unlike thinking about it or picturing it in our minds. Nonetheless, we must consider that spirit and matter may be two sides of a more general and more unified reality.

The best argument for the unity of spirit and matter is given by Teilhard de Chardin, the Jesuit paleontologist, and we will find it is also backed up by modern physics. He says that if conscious and spiritualized beings have evolved within the realm of matter, then the potential for that spiritualization must be present in matter, even in its most primitive forms. That is, if we conceive of matter as made up of elementary determinisms, which would be the case for matter without spirit, we "block all roads that would bring us to the present state of the universe." Evolution would be impossible. "On the other hand, . . . a cosmos initially made up of *elementary freedoms*. . . has the necessary elasticity" not only to allow and account for evolution, but also to yield the predictability and precision which we experience in the physical sciences. This matter, made up of elementary freedoms, he calls "spirit-matter." (1969, p. 23)

If matter in its primitive forms exhibits this freedom as a "molecule of the spirit," what shall we say of the other end of the spectrum where we envision spirit as a great unifying and patterning principle which guides evolution? That would be pure spirit if anything could be so called. If we may say that there is no matter without spirit, must we not also say that there is no spirit without matter? The *symmetry* of the situation demands that we acknowledge the possibility that this is so.

It is *not* a case, as Teilhard says, of matter *becoming* spirit, but rather of spirit-matter gradually fulfilling more and more of its potential. One might be tempted to say its *spiritual* potential, but one must be careful to keep the balance: spirit is fulfilled in matter.

We must always be aware of both sides of the affirmation that there is no matter without spirit and no spirit without matter. It has seemed that there are two aspects of spirit: one in the process of emergence within the complexification of organic forms, and one seeming to descend into matter from a source beyond. Isn't this latter spirit without matter? Is not God, at least, conceived as apart from matter? Or, what might be the corresponding matter?

It may be the cosmos as a whole. Upon reflection this is the obvious place to look. The spirit descending seems to come from an infinite sea of potentiality, but this is also and always the potentiality of organic interconnections inherent in the tiniest material particles. It comes out of a *totality* and the cosmos is such a totality. The implication is not only that the material in one's immediate vicinity is effective in shaping local interconnections, but also that which is "at a distance."

If the whole cosmos somehow participates in guiding the evolution of each of its parts, then we may well find that our guiding fact, the evolution of consciousness out of that which is unconscious, is not merely local but is occurring throughout the cosmos. Again, that which is unconscious in the cosmos consists of the totality of the original hydrogen atoms produced as protons and electrons in the Big Bang. Our task is to see how this primal "stuff of the universe" can evolve into the organic forms needed to support consciousness.

Astronomers know quite well how stellar processes produce the whole range of chemical elements from hydrogen, and other sciences can pretty well detail the further development of these elements into living, evolving organisms, even if they cannot say exactly how or why. The evidence for the continuity of the whole evolutionary process is strong.

Though consciousness is not a *property* of primordial matter, it seems to be a *potential* of the primary stuff. That which is unconscious also includes all the potentialities for evolutionary development, which together make up an aspect of primordial spirit. Human consciousness is neither matter nor spirit exclusively but lies between and unites those polar opposites. In the beginning was spirit-matter and now also is spirit-matter, but where there was not consciousness there now is consciousness.

The Relatedness of Opposites

Insofar as *conscious* and *unconscious* are opposites, the evolution of the one out of the other gives us the prime example of the relatedness of opposites. Where there is the logical discontinuity of the two terms, there is still their factual continuity via the evolutionary process.

This relatedness of certain opposites in physics is called *complementarity,* which Edward Teller describes as follows:

> The idea of complementarity is that in order to describe a situation you have to use (at least on certain occasions) two mutually exclusive approaches. If you omit either, the description is incomplete. Both must be used. Because they are mutually exclusive, it is necessary to adjust the two approaches in a manner that is by no means obvious. (Teller, 1969, p. 83)

Although complementarity in physics draws certain opposites—certain physical quantities or concepts—together, it does not apply to *all* physical quantities. It singles out pairs whose measurement simultaneously would require conflicting experimental conditions. Yet behind the measurement situation lie the descriptive concepts of the quantities to be measured. Thus problems of measurement are ultimately conceptual problems of description, and the principle of complementarity states that a complete description sometimes required conflicting attributes, such as wave and particle. Since the model of complementarity seems capable of application to many situations beyond physics,[1] it will be discussed at some length in Chapter Four.

This relationship of conscious and unconscious also elucidates the nature of the role of the observer in the study of matter. This will be the topic of Chapter Three. Physicists employ human consciousness, the conscious aspect of nature, to study the unconscious "stuff" out of which that consciousness evolved. Because our guiding fact establishes the continuity of the observer and the observed, we might expect our concepts to apply quite precisely to the atomic and subatomic "particles" of which we are made. But as conscious and unconscious are also logically *discontinuous*, we expect and, indeed, find that our concepts do *not* apply. If we could expect only precise applicability, we could probably deduce the so-called laws of physics by means of pure thought, but because our concepts do not apply in an unambiguous way, observation is necessary. Strictly speaking, our concepts *can* be applied to the description and behavior of fundamental entities, but logically contradictory concepts *also* apply, and only observation can help us describe a given situation. Moreover, we are forced to choose which of the two contradictory aspects we want to know about most precisely. Not all physicists take kindly to this situation. Einstein was one of those

---

1. This is demonstrated in *A Comparison of 'Complementarity' in Quantum Physics with Analogous Structures in Kierkegaard's Philosophical Writings, From a Jungian Point of View*, the author's doctoral dissertation. (Hitchcock, 1976)

who maintained that pure thought would still find a way to reason out the laws of nature without resorting to observations.

However, again, human concepts, even mathematical ones, are descriptions and not facts. We can, for instance, describe the evolution of a star by means of mathematical equations, but a star does not do any mathematics. The so-called laws of physics are not what govern the cosmos, but are only our attempts to describe that which does govern it.

Another aspect of the inapplicability of our concepts to the microphysical realm is the fact that all of these concepts are derived from everyday experience. Our highly evolved ability to perceive depends on complex organs which are of what we might call a middle size, between the size of atoms and that of the cosmos. The concepts which we acquire out of sensory experience apply quite well to our experience of midsized objects but not to the supersmall or superlarge. We have seen that with the advent of sufficient complexity in evolution, opposites and contradictions can emerge. This aspect of the inapplicability of our concepts, then, is really the same as the previous one.

Whatever knowledge we have is human knowledge—*characteristically* human knowledge—and as such is limited. It is limited by its rationality and even by its wealth of detail. It is limited by the fact that we cannot observe without disturbing the behavior, and even the nature, of that which is being observed. But above all, it is limited by the unlikeness of the microphysical and cosmic realms which it desires to describe. We can assert that "God knows," perhaps, but that does not help us and eventually we must conclude, with Scheibe (1973), that "knowledge known to none is no knowledge."

THE STUFF OF THE UNIVERSE

At this point we are interested in two aspects of evolution which have arisen in considering the guiding fact. First, physics tells us much about the primordial "stuff" out of which consciousness evolved. "Stuff" is a term employed by Teilhard de Chardin to avoid using the word "matter." As he says, using the same guiding fact, "The stuff of the Universe is spirit-matter; no other substance than this could produce the human molecule" (1969, p. 58). This will be the topic of Chapter Five. Secondly, we can also perceive the very continuity of the evolutionary process which links human consciousness with the unconscious primordial stuff.

With regard to this stuff, we find remarkable confirmation that the principle of the relatedness of opposites is quite general. When we examine the simplest stable forms of stuff, the protons and electrons which are the building blocks of atoms, we encounter what is known as wave-particle duality. In our attempts to describe these entities accurately we find that sometimes they are best described as wavelike and sometimes as particle-like, but these two descriptions are logically incompatible. We also encounter the same duality in the description of light and other electromagnetic phenomena. The word *particle* is a term descriptive of entities which are essentially separated or discontinuous from their surroundings. Fundamental particles are indivisible (unless their basic identity is sacrificed) and can be put in a box. Boxability means that one can state that absolutely all of the particle is within certain spatial boundaries. Waves, on the other hand, are essentially continuous and of infinite extent, while the stuff of which they are made is essentially divisible without sacrifice of identity. Particles are discontinuous (indivisible and boxable); waves are continuous (divisible and unboxable).

Again, we have the separation of opposites (the particle nature), as in the logical distinction between conscious and unconscious, and we have the continuity (the wave nature), as in the evolutionary process by which the conscious evolves out of the unconscious. We may note that with the wave nature of entities, the question whether action at a distance is possible becomes moot, for in that sense there is no distance between entities.

Still considering the evolving stuff, we now encounter the ideas of spirit and matter. From the particle aspect arises the notion of a definite amount of something, a quantity of matter which, to physicists, signifies both its inertia or resistance to acceleration, and its gravitational ability to attract other matter. With the wave aspect we discover patterning and dynamics which I identify as spirit. There is much discussion in this book of this use of the word *spirit*, and I find it answers well to common usage at all points. With the essential unity of the incompatible opposites of wave and particle in real stuff, we therefore also have the essential unity of spirit and matter. Thus we follow Teilhard in designating this stuff as spirit-matter.

Moving, then, to the evolution of spirit-matter (the topic of Chapter Six), it is possible to trace the development of detail and specificity in the patterns seen in the simplest form of spirit-matter, the hydrogen atom. In particular, we can see steps in this evolution by looking at several stages of complexity from hydrogen atoms, to snowflakes, to brains. When pictures of snowflakes are shown next to those of models of hydrogen atoms (see pages 138 and 143), the similarities in their shapes are seen to be quite remarkable. Snowflakes look like hydrogen atoms with the details filled in. The lobes of the brain likewise show resemblance through the predominance of small whole numbers (six major cerebral lobes, six branches of a snowflake, six lobes in some hydrogen atom patterns). The hydrogen atoms also resemble "God-images" such as Jung described by means of mandalas. Thus, the evolutionary growth in complexity from atoms, to snowflakes, to brains might well be described as an evolving image of God. Hence the title *Atoms, Snowflakes, and God*. And since the God-image guides the evolutionary process from within as well as from without the evolving matter, it is no surprise to find fresh expressions of the God-image in the images from the human unconscious which have flowed from inspired individuals.

In describing this development of detail, use is made of the analogies found in the photographic science of holography, wherein each tiny piece of a hologram contains the entire scene photographed, but with less detail the smaller the piece. A major point in the development of detail is the emergence of functions which were certainly included in the potentials of spirit-matter from the beginning but which were hardly foreseeable by those organisms in which the evolution was progressing. Among these functions is the one with which this chapter began, namely, consciousness. If this function was continuously in preparation in evolution, then we must take teleological views seriously, at least in certain forms. Human consciousness is ego-consciousness and it is always consciousness *of something*. Some sort of image or idea of the something is related to the ego or "I" in such a way that the ego is aware of the object.

It is interesting to note that ego-consciousness of particulars may be called a polar opposite of omniscience, in that omniscience is not limited by the prerequisite of the "I" or ego. Omniscience is more like the potentials of the patterning to fill in detail by means of evolution. The possibility of water, for example, is present in pure hydrogen even before the oxygen component of water has evolved from hydrogen in stellar interiors. This possibility is not represented to any consciousness in the early stages of the cosmos, and yet is somehow, as we might say, foreseen to omniscience.

To carry this idea further into the realm of functions of the psyche, we may take the human brain as a central example. Paleontologists tell us that a cranial capacity of around 1300 cubic centimeters is required for the self-awareness or self-reflexivity which is one of the hallmarks of true humanity. At a time when the precursors of the genus *Homo* had a brain of, say, half that volume, it still was developing *toward* that human function. From hindsight we can say that the continued growth and differentiation of that brain were following an *entelechy* or goal-directedness leading to reflexive thought, and that it was the *sort* of organ in which thought might emerge. At the present, correspondingly, we are undoubtedly unable to perceive the possible human functions still to be actualized. It is the idea of *holographic evolution* which regrounds the notion of a teleological thrust.

We may note in passing that the relatedness, even the unity, of logical opposites cannot be *rationally* encompassed. Thus, if things are this way, the way the *facts* indicate, both the opposites of rational and nonrational must be included in a suprarational process in reality. The rational is one side of the process, namely the particularizing or categorizing side, and the other, corresponding to the wave is nonrational, inclusive, interactive.

GOD IN HUMAN KNOWLEDGE

At one time the intended title of this book was *The Theology of Complementarity*. The change to the present title was necessitated, in addition to the reasons already given by the impression which the word *theology* makes on people. It seems to have an overwhelming Christian connotation and therefore lacks the breadth it would have as a word on its own, based only on the root meanings of its elements. Of itself, *theology* designates that which can be rationally known of the nature of God. According to this general sense, this present book has many theological implications. Therefore it seems important here to say in what sense the book is theological.

In religious experience "God" is felt or perceived in, or as, what Otto (1958) called the numinous. This term designates that part of the meaning of the word *holy* which is purely nonrational and which is specifically nonmoral. It is entirely an experiential term, referring to what Otto called the experience of Awe or *Mysterium Tremendum*. As he also implied, the experience makes any explanation unnecessary, and without the experience no explanation can suffice. When one has experienced the Numinous, he or she will say, with C, G, Jung, "I don't need to believe [in God], I *know*."

However, not every numinous experience can be attributed directly to God. In fact, if one asks the question of any experience whether or not it is so attributable—asks it with sufficient intellectual sharpness—it will turn out that the rational side of the mind cannot maintain the conviction which holds for the nonrational side: the experience is *never* rationally attributable, for through various causes we explain it away or dismiss it. This is partly due, among other causes, to the personal nature of such experiences, coupled with our need to resort to consensus for the establishing of "fact," and partly due to the fact that the terms into which one attempts to put the experience for the asking of the question defy a satisfying link to godhead.

If we were to remain here, we would, of course, be left without any sort of theology insofar as the root word *logos* applies toward bringing the rational side itself to the question of the being of God. Thus, the very word *theology* is a paradox, not merely the paradox that words or concepts are used in an attempt to describe everyday actions and objects, the experience of the experimental physicist, or the experience of normal thoughts and emotions, but that words are used in an attempt to describe the experience of the numinous by the individual. Thus in the fact that we use the word *theology* we do have empirical data on the fact of the existence and conflict of the rational and the nonrational faculties in humans. Both of these faculties are phenomena of the psyche—two dispositions which are tendencies to say, respectively, "God is dead" and "God is alive." Yet both of these statements assume the experience of the numinous. Without this experience, the rational says, "There is no God" (no intellectual need for such an hypothesis), and the nonrational says, "Life is meaningless," for in general it is the quality of numinous experience which conveys a sense of meaning to individual lives. (I am well aware of the extreme oversimplification of these last statements.)

Yet the experience without the concept is not yet a

concretion. One might well say it does not yet exist, thus defining existence in a very profitable way, for it is always a balance of contradictory opposites. A personal experience cannot be communicated, cannot form part of a field of study unless it is somehow captured in interpersonal terms, i.e., a common language with reasonably well-defined commonsense concepts. Niels Bohr has stated the same situation in physics:

> . . . It is decisive to recognize that, *however far the phenomena transcend the scope of classical physical explanation, the account of all evidence must be expressed in classical terms.* The argument is simply that by the word 'experiment' we refer to a situation where we can tell others what we have done and what we have learned and that, therefore, the account of the experimental arrangement and of the results of the observations must be expressed in unambiguous language with suitable application of the terminology of classical physics. (Bohr, 1963, p. 39)

Still, numinous experience often carries with it a passionate desire for communication. It is as if it is in its nature to be inclusive of others, though it can only be, in its essence as experience, in the individual. Physicist Michael Polanyi describes a similar situation in the field of scientific discovery in the following terms:

> Just as mechanical forces are the gradients of a potential energy, so this field of forces (mental unease that seeks appeasement of itself) would also be the gradient of a potentiality; a gradient arising from the proximity of a possible achievement. . .(the discoverer) senses the proximity of something unknown and strives passionately towards it. . .Yet all the time the creative

> mind is searching for something believed to be
> real; which, being real, will—when discovered—
> be entitled to claim universal validity—something
> the knowledge of which must indeed passionately
> insist on its own universal validity. (Polyani, 1962,
> pp. 398, 395-396)

Here, in advance, is a case where the Greater Inclusive includes the separativeness of the concept for the sake of totality, and with a *risk*, for the experience can come into existence demonically as well as in love.

The Value of Separateness

So then we have the fact of consciousness having arisen out of the unconscious *as a product* of the tendency toward particles, toward differentiation and specificity, and, which is the same thing, toward the purposeful evolution of individuals. In this process our conscious side has become very seriously separated from even our own unconscious side, and much more so from our universal ground. We as individuals are much more self-contained or particulate than members of a tribe. And most of us no longer have vital contact with the internal God-image. It was the sum of these separations which Tillich (1948) called "sin," especially where we are aware of and participate in these separations. And when individuals experience the reconnection, we, with Tillich, call these experiences "grace." The word religion means precisely reconnection, and I am suggesting that both the need and the process are much more universal than has been generally recognized. Various religions, both Western and Eastern, have had their own approaches to the primal world of connectedness, but again the suggestion here is that religion is not a matter of specific practices. The religious need is an expression of the essential interconnectedness of all things, of spirit, matter, and psyche, in and through the guiding image of evolution which I have called the God-image.

The God-image is not defined except in terms of the aggregate of images which have been seen as god-images by humans. It thus combines essentially all opposites. Moreover, the religious need in humans is a product of the separation itself. This means that innocence needs no religious experience, for it is a nonreligious state. This is perhaps the most inscrutable aspect of the purposiveness of the evolution of consciousness, that consciousness itself is a wound in the primal unity. At the same time, if evolution is holographically guided, the development of consciousness is purposeful and so also is the separation which requires reconciliation.

Consciousness is the medium for the existence of knowledge, and that knowledge is of two kinds, the rational and the nonrational. As the concepts of particle and wave are both needed for a complete description of physical entities, so scientific and religious knowledge are both needed to describe the total reality of the cosmos: spirit, matter, and psyche.

It is to be hoped that clarity about this fact will assist the next needed step in evolution: that the ego shed its attitude of rationalistic radical separatism, because it is not the ultimate truth in the patterning, and consciously allow itself to be grasped by the total purposiveness of the patterning. This will be the true convergence of science and religion.

2

Reality, Being, Existence

In the beginning, in the small and the great darkness, life is not Something; it ardently is. Beginnings are not precision. Beginnings are not confusion. They are darkness drawn to a minute point of nondarkness, and silence gathered into a small sound. What is gathered and drawn together, and who gathers and focuses, lies behind knowledge. We can only know, as we peer into the mystery, that it is so.

Sheila Moon, A Magic Dwells

What is it to begin in the middle? The whole evolution of the cosmos has gone on for perhaps fifteen billion years. Now we are just on the verge of being able to say what the conditions of its beginnings were and what its future development may be. It is expanding. Some say it will expand forever, but others say it will collapse to a small object of extreme density in sixty to eighty billion years. If we can make better observations of its present state, we will be able to say much more about its past and future.

In this cosmos life developed from that which was nonliving and consciousness from that which was unconscious. Have we exhausted the potentials of the cosmos for evolving new things? If we can fill in the details of evolution and see how it is possible that a new phenomenon can emerge, we may be able to see more deeply the future of conscious life.

That sciences may begin in the middle with facts rather than with axioms was brought out in the last chapter. Of course, just as we desire to discover the *what* of our physical beginnings and the future of the cosmos, we want to be able to discern *why* things are as they are. We desire not only to push back the curtains of time, but also to discover the properties of the smallest and most fundamental constituents of this cosmos in hope of some clues as to the *why*. Does it begin from first *principles*, from first *particles*, from both, or from something entirely other? At each level of discovery, that which we thought might be a clue to the why turns out to be only another what. Slowly we work our way back and down and in. But so great is the gap between our size and that of the fundamental entities that we can no more stand at that beginning than we can at the beginning of time.

Yet we try to apply our concepts as well as we can. Among these concepts are three which are of a different order from those used specifically in physical description such as particle, wave, mass, length, time, and electric charge. Nevertheless, these three, reality, being, and existence, hold a key to the point of view of beginning in the middle, even if they are not yet specific descriptions. In ordinary usage, even by physicists, they are either left vague or they are employed in ways which deny that we do in fact begin in the middle.

Therefore we must put aside pure description for the time being and define these terms from the inside, as it were. After these definitions, it will be possible to define a fourth term, *phenomenon*, which will bring us much closer to knowing *what* it is we are trying to describe. Is it an objective "thing-in-itself" *(ding an sich)*, or is it more intimately bound up with us as the ones who would know what it is? This question is central in microphysics as suggested by the epigraph to Chapter One. "Knowledge known to none is no knowledge."

REALITY

Most approaches to a definition of reality attempt to define the term in and of itself, employing such notions as permanence, causal priority, efficaciousness, thing-likeness, and logical necessity. In doing so, such approaches yield definitions that simply ignore the fact that all knowledge—in fact, everything which is conscious to us—is psychic in nature. By this is meant that all contents of consciousness reside in, and are components of, the psyche. We can observe our physiology and note that when, for instance, nerve impulses are sent from the eye to the brain, something synthesizes these numerous impulses into an *image*, i.e., imparts unity to them. To say that the impulses are somehow *mediated* to the psyche or become psychic is the same thing. Hume allowed for the psychic nature of knowledge when he said that "impressions of sensation...arise in the soul originally from unknown causes," but he disallowed any origin beyond the soul or psyche. Jung wrote that such impressions at least come *through* the psyche:

> It is an almost ridiculous prejudice to assume that existence can only be physical. As a matter of fact the only form of existence of which we have immediate knowledge is psychic. We might well say, on the contrary, that physical existence is a mere inference, since we know matter only insofar as we perceive psychic images mediated by the senses. (Jung 1969b, p. 12)

It would seem then that just as it is impossible to

divorce knowledge of the physical world from the knower, it is impossible to divorce abstract concepts such as "reality" from the psyche. What is real impresses us with its reality, whether its origin is in the inner world or the outer. The simple fact is that reality is experienced and defined by the ego and is "objective reality" only in relation to the ego. It is never "objective reality in itself" as known or even as clearly defined. The terms I and not-I, used for the subject and object respectively, are especially useful for keeping this fact in mind because the "I" is the reference point in both. As long as we attempt to define reality as absolutely distinct from an experiencing subject, we are bound to fall into one pit or another. Actually it is the same pit under various possible guises, such as the conception of God as "absolutely other," the idea that "the laws of physics are free inventions of the human intellect" (Einstein), or that there is a totally unbridgeable gulf between the world of concepts and the empirical world of sense impressions. These three statements are all forms of the single assumption that there is an absolutely distinct objective reality which either may (Einstein) or may not (Kant) be known via pure thought. It is one of the tasks of this book to show not only what the bridge is between psyche and nonpsyche (or spirit/matter), but also to demonstrate the bridge between the two perceivable forms of the nonpsychic, i.e. between spirit and matter.

There are those for whom the solid object is most real and those who feel or think that the "first cause," or spirit or God, is most real.

Many have felt that the "ultimate reality" must be a nonphysical realm of both causes and ends, i.e., that ultimate reality is spirit. This is because (1) physical reality has been so hard to define; and/or (2) because of the assumption that the obvious presence of evil in the world-as-experienced seems to make necessary a world beyond in which things are better or purer, and/or for other reasons as well.

On the other hand, many have felt that while matter may or may not be *ultimate* reality, it is as ultimate as reality can be. This is because of (1) matter's tangibility, intractability and obvious physical power, and/or (2) its durability as exemplified in atomic nuclei and in the cosmos itself; and/or (3) because it is at least relatively more definable than spirit. Also some have gone in thought beyond knowable reality to an ultimate physical reality, namely, the thing-in-itself which is totally other than our knowledge of it.

Obviously both spirit and matter seem real to humans, and we usually are suspended between these poles. Both of them "work" or are efficacious in some sense, even though we don't know spirit or matter in any ultimate sense. We are in the middle and must begin there to explore the frontiers. What we know and experience consists of many psychic images which, however, speak to us of two realms: one of spirit, the other of matter.

These realms seem real and *are* real precisely because they impose limitations upon us. I cannot walk through an ordinary wall; therefore, the physical is real. I cannot manipulate my vision or dream. It grips me and is therefore real. The wall and the dream are relatively hard realities. Once we learn what is difficult or impossible to manipulate, perhaps we can refine our sense of reality to include the more subtle forms of limitation in which our participation changes the state of things. The piece of paper was no less real because I was able to tear it in two, and the contract was no less real because I was able to break it.

Let us, then, try out the following: (1) the ego is the subject of reality, and (2) reality is the imposition of limitation. The first statement means that "reality" is a *psychic* designation or descriptive term, i.e., a category of experience. It also means that the ego is the subject of reality valuation, which is to say that ego makes such valuations. What, then, may be said of the reality of the ego and of its participation in objective reality? (And let us remember that objective does *not* mean *absolutely* objective.) Here we must consider the ego in its collective aspect; its definition both via interaction with other humans and also through its experience of limitation in the world. This problem is part of a more general problem regarding the psyche as its own point of reference, which is explained within the point of view of complementarity, as will be shown later. Reality as imposition of limitation *upon* the ego in no way denies the objectivity or reality of the ego itself. In fact, as the imposition of limitation, the gaining of the sense of reality implies activity on the part of the ego. We do not discover what reality is without probing the boundaries. *Reality* is thus the imposition of limitation *at the limit of the push for expansion.*

The compatibility of this definition of reality with Jung's definition of *psyche* is evident from the following:

> What I would call the psyche proper extends to all functions which can be brought under the influence of a will. Pure instinctuality allows no consciousness to be conjectured and needs none. But because of its empirical freedom of choice, the will needs a supra-ordinate authority, some-

thing like a consciousness of itself, in order to modify the (instinctual) function. It must 'know' of a goal different from the goal of the function. Volition presupposes a choosing subject who envisages different possibilities.... What I am trying to make clear is the remarkable fact that the will cannot transgress the bonds of the psychic sphere: it cannot coerce the instinct, nor has it power over the spirit, insofar as we understand by this something more than the intellect. Spirit and instinct are by nature autonomous and both limit in equal measure the applied field of the will. (Jung 1969c, p. 183)

The above definition also implies that a sense of limitation or finitude, discovered by humans via a process of expansive exploration, is necessary in order to ask the question of what reality is, a view which is parallel to that of Tillich's regarding "being."

If man is that being who asks the question of being, he has and has not the being for which he asks. He is separated from it while belonging to it.... Our power of being is limited.... This is precisely what is meant when we say that we are finite. He who is infinite *does* not ask.... and a being which does not realize that it is finite *cannot* ask. (Tillich 1964, p. 11)

We perceive limitations that are *effective* limitations, but whose ultimate nature we do not know. The point is that with the above definition we do not need to know the ultimate nature either of spiritual reality or of physical reality, but we can define them based upon the two basic kinds of limitation which we experience. We must attempt to describe that which we *can* know. Humans resist the idea of *any* limitation and want to feel that there is nothing which we can't know in principle. Such an attitude refuses to face and acknowledge human finitude, at least as a distinct and clearly present side of our total being.

The difference between those kinds of reality which we call "physical" or "spiritual" is also illuminated by the phrase, "limitation at the end of the push for expansion." Physical reality is often easily accepted, or at least we are clear about it. I do not try continually to walk through a wall. It is in the less tangible areas of understanding, motivation, relationships, dreams, and the like, that limitation is less clearly perceived and less easily accepted. These latter, then, in part define spiritual reality.

That which imposes limitations on the I (or ego) is, by definition, the *not-I*—that over which my will exercises no control. This *not-I*, as experienced, is already psychic even in the case of physiological stimuli of which the ego becomes conscious. It is the dramatic *difference* between the approximately somatic limitations (products of the senses) and the approximately psychic limitations (conceptual, emotional, spiritual), as experienced, that justifies the mind-body duality which, according to the Swiss psychologist Aniela Jaffe, finds its extreme in the duality of spirit-matter. Many thinkers have ascribed the greatest reality either to spirit or to matter one-sidedly. Therefore, having made the precautionary statement that both are included as impinging on the psychic realm—which is the only place where they are perceived—we may profitably deal with them separately.

PHYSICAL REALITY

According to Jung the ego is not present at birth—the *I* develops as the *not-I* is experienced. The infantile or primitive psyche is quite diffuse, which is to say that its contents and potentialities are "projected" onto all of its surroundings. Hence the first experiences of reality are bodily differentiations of *I* from *not-I*: bodily *will* terminates at the skin, beyond which are objects much less susceptible of change according to the person's desires. There, too, the sense of touch terminates. Limitation in the form of the "real world" of objects is encountered.

With exercise of the senses, correlation of sense impressions, and the increase of knowledge, the "real world" becomes a highly refined concept. For example, at the adult level the phrase "he needs to accept the real world" expresses the same sense of *limitation* but in a much more complex form, involving, not the existence of material objects, but the difference between fantasy and work. As part of the same development the body itself becomes a highly differentiated *object* for the ego, though there always remains a fringe area wherein one doubts the objectivity of a symptom, i.e., doubts that it is of physiological origin. We may indeed interpret a real (limiting) event incorrectly without jeopardizing our knowledge that a real event has occurred. Here we find the notion that our concepts (and physical laws) are approximately correct to be quite useful: our knowledge of the real may be imprecise, but we know *that* we are dealing with the real.

In the realm of the apparati of physical science the same holds true. We do not receive direct sensory experience of, say, an electron, but we have devised experiments in a continuous range of refinements which can respond to what we then *name* as a single electron. Our experiments do not show just *any* result but definite (limited) results. Again our *model* of this reality may need refinement or may actually be inadequate, but the *reality* of the electron is not thereby called into question.

Thus the range of physical reality includes three major modes of presenting images to the ego: internal stimuli, stimuli from external sources, stimuli from instruments which require associated models. Internal stimuli are directly presented by internal physiological stimuli via conversion into one or more psychic images (by an as yet unspecifed process), which images can be apperceived by the ego (such as all bodily awareness). Stimuli from external sources are received from without the body, converted by bodily senses into physiological stimuli, and thence to psychic images apperceivable by the ego (such as awareness of surroundings). Stimuli which are converted by instruments (in a reliable way) into a situation can be grasped by the senses (as in the case of "pointer readings") and thence brought to ego awareness by the sequence of transformations just mentioned.

SPIRITUAL REALITY

Spiritual reality is exemplified in the realm of image by dreams, visions, and visual memory of scenes from physical reality; in the realm of concept by intuitions and verbally based thought processes; and in the realm of affect by emotions which seem to impress themselves unavoidably upon us.

Thinking about something is, in experience, vastly different from touching the thing. In similar ways we usually can distinguish well enough the nonmaterial from the physical impressions, though it is possible to counterfeit physical impressions by stimulating nerve tissues by which real physical impressions would be mediated to the psyche. Examples are the sense of having a real limb even after amputation, or evoking sense impressions by electrically stimulating the brain. Nevertheless, normal experience justifies a consideration of two clearly distinguished classes of limitations, spiritual and physical.

We usually agree that physical reality is nonpsychic in itself and must be mediated to the psyche, but we have so identified with spirit that it is much less clear to us that spiritual reality is also nonpsychic and, equally with physical reality, requires mediation.

This leads naturally to a consideration of what spirit *is*, which will entail a brief digression from the main trend of thought concerning reality. Nevertheless, the following few pages on the distinction between spiritual reality and psychic reality (parallel to the distinction between physical reality and psychic reality) will help clarify the nature of psychic reality and will set the stage for making clear the interaction of physical and spiritual reality and the transcendental unity of these two in what Jung called "archetypal" reality.

In order to see what is meant by spirit, we may have recourse to a personal anecdote which describes one of the most formative moments for this book. As background for that moment, let us look at the following statement by astronomer Martin Schwarzschild:

> If simple and perfect laws uniquely rule the universe, should not pure thought be capable of uncovering this perfect set of laws without having to lean on the crutches of tediously assembled observations? (Schwarzschild 1958, p. 1)

This is a high philosophical ideal whose clearest enunciator was Kant. However, in the beauty of the language many assumptions lie hidden. What do *simple* and *perfect* mean, for instance? Rationally simple, or simple in some other way? One goal of Zen meditation is a simplicity which lies definitely beyond rationality. And T. S. Eliot describes for humans, "a condition of complete simplicity, costing not less than everything." It is certainly a higher order simplicity which describes that which "rules the universe," not a rational, formally simple mathematical law. Physicist Richard Feynman in his Nobel prize acceptance lecture has given a possible definition of simplicity for physics which shows the same distinction:

> It always seems odd to me that the fundamental laws of physics, when discovered, can appear in so many forms that are not apparently identical at first. I don't know what it means, that nature chooses these curious forms, but maybe that is a way of defining simplicity. Perhaps a thing is simple if you can describe it fully in several different ways without immediately knowing that you are describing the same thing. (Feynman 1966, p. 702)

What is "pure thought"? Here an ultimate simplicity of concept is presumed which isn't the case, as is discussed in Chapter Three. Again, Kant is responsible for the mind-set of modern philosophers which falsely holds that every complex concept is a compound of simples and can be "unpacked" to reveal its fundamental rational components. In truth, every empirical concept is fundamentally indefinable in purely rational terms, a situation which is parallel to the case of the "electron" and "photon" of modern physics, which will be discussed in Chapter Four.

But now to the story. I was in a course on stellar structure. On the day in question Professor Henyey was discussing the difficulty of finding solutions to the four simultaneous, second-order differential equations which together form the basis of the study of stellar structure. These equations cannot be solved by analytical means, but only through successive numerical approximation: try one set of assumptions, see how it fits, adjust and try again with different numbers. But, in emphasizing that a solution must exist because the star exists, he said, "After all, the star must solve these equations." As many statements just float by when one is concentrating on following the main argument, so did this one. Some might pounce on it immediately, but it only gradually dawned upon me that a star doesn't solve equations in any sense at all—it just *is*. It has no problem being a star, no will, no consciousness. The equations that express the laws of physics are just descriptions of something.

If we look back to the previous quotation from Feynman, we can see the same sort of thing. Here are all these seemingly diverse descriptions of the same phenomena, each of which is adequate in itself, but the phenomena *as such* are somehow different. Perhaps one could say that it is a pattern or patterning which is being described by the mathematical equations. There is an organizing and patterning quality at work in physical reality but it seems to be the patterning itself, rather than reason, which carries it. Reason can only attempt to describe it. A major shift in thought is needed: *The laws of physics do not govern the universe; rather they are our attempts to describe that which does govern the universe.* This is one answer to Schwarzschild, as quoted above, but not a complete answer. It requires yet some statement of the necessity of observation, which will be given in Chapter Three.

Now the question arises: what then *does* govern?

What are we attempting and always failing to describe? It is not matter itself, but some set of conditions not rationally tractable, yet simple in a higher sense, which moves and forms matter in and into observable relations. It is a patterning. Is this what we call spirit? The step of identifying spirit with patterning took years, but with further study and discussion it made more and more sense. Two crucial pieces of input to this process were Teilhard's association of the idea of "elementary freedoms" with the behavior of atoms, and the photographs of mathematically derived models of hydrogen atoms, which physicist Harvey White published in 1931, both of which are discussed in Chapter Five.

We have disidentified with matter and have identified with spirit, and therefore philosophy does not recognize the barrier of indescribability which lies between ego-consciousness and spirit. However, our concepts are reflections in the psyche of something which is not in itself psychic. Just as matter is not psychic in itself, the same must be said of spirit. Just as the effects of physical occurrences arrive at our brain as nerve impulses (considerably preprocessed by our physiology) which must be somehow translated into psychic images compatible with consciousness, so also our very concepts are psychic images of a preconceptual, preperceptual patterning, or as von Franz says, of a "transcendental background." Yet somehow this background is *psychoid*, meaning that there is sufficient similarity for it to be mediated to the psyche.

For Kant, the transcendental realm contained rational, clear, necessary, and universal concepts and relations, while for Jung and von Franz it is nonrational. In fact, this background for them is equally the source of what we perceive as matter as it is of spirit. It is the *unus mundus*, the unitary source of all natural opposites. The psyche perceives its grounding as bipolar: spirit and matter.

Thus we may picture spiritual and physical reality in relation to the psyche, which contains the ego, as follows:

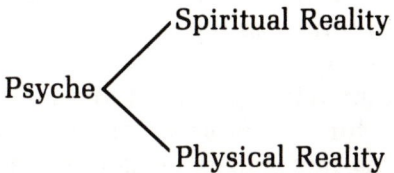

Psyche — Spiritual Reality / Physical Reality

But behind the apparent duality of spirit and matter is a unitary transcendental reality, so that the picture becomes:

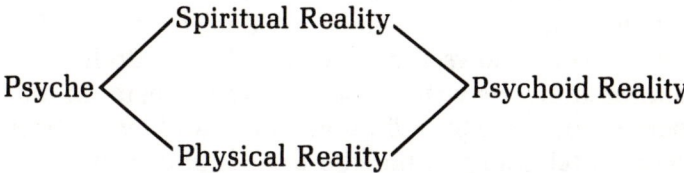

Psyche — Spiritual Reality \ Physical Reality — Psychoid Reality

The psychoid reality is often called "archetypal reality," for we may infer various archetypal components of the psychoid. That is, the psychoid is not absolutely unitary in the sense that it has no discernable components, but in the sense that each of the archetypes brings opposites (i.e., spirit and matter) together. Beyond the distinguishable archetypes, however, all archetypes merge into a God-image, or an image of an ultimate reality, which is thus truly unitary.

The God-image is often experienced in forms which combine the circle and the cross, as in mandala symbolism where the ultimate unity is represented by the circle which contains and encloses a cross. The presence of the cross shows that even the tendency to separate into distinguishable elements has its origin in the overarching unity.

Thus, if the fundamental guiding fact is the case and that which is conscious has evolved out of that which is unconscious, from both poles of spirit and matter, psyche is a potential of the primordial ingredients of the cosmos, and the term *psychoid* truly applies to the original "stuff."

It is well known that purely random processes cannot account for the rapidity of evolution on this planet. In this fact and from documented cases of that which Jung calls "synchronicity," we have evidence that the transcendental patterning organizes spirit and matter simultaneously. Synchronicity is the occurrence of an outer event which coincides with, or brings to consciousness, the *meaning* of a moment or a time for an individual or group. The outer event shows the inner condition. Both spirit and matter, however opposed they seem in our perceptions, are brought together in and by the transcendental background, the *unus mundus*. It is important to note also that they are brought together in the perceptions of the psyche. This is an example of the function exhibited in the diagram above. In this sense we may say that they are brought together *again* in the psyche, for in the *unus mundus* they *are* together.

It was indeed the participation of matter in processes otherwise designated as spirit that prompted Jung to adapt the term *psychoid* to the description of spirit-matter. The psyche stands between two poles.[1]

---

1. For Jung's discussion of these poles see *The Structure and Dynamics of the Psyche* (1969c), pp. 175-78, 183f, 205f, and *Archetypes of the Collective Unconscious* (1969a), p. 173.

At the lower end—the "psychic infrared"—volition, the criterion of psyche, merges with instinct which is grounded in physiology and ultimately in the nature of carbon. At the upper end—the "psychic ultraviolet"—the will again is up against something which it cannot coerce or manipulate: something with the ability to "organize images and ideas" and objects as well, and which also manifests itself as numinous. Of this something, Jung said, "this aspect deserves the epithet 'spiritual' above all else."

> What I am trying to make clear is the remarkable fact that the will cannot transgress the bounds of the psychic sphere: it cannot coerce the instinct, nor has it power over the spirit, insofar as we understand by this something more than the intellect. Spirit and instinct are by nature autonomous and both limit in equal measure the applied field of the will. (Jung, 1969c, p 183)

Jung's remarks apply most closely to the ranges of spirit and matter that are contiguous with psyche. In other places he extends the application of the psychoid to the ultimate nature of things, as has been shown by Jaffe in *The Myth of Meaning* (1979) and in *Out of the Life and Work of C. G. Jung* (1971). By means of the term *psychoid*, he refers to the tendency of the cosmos to produce psyche evolutionarily.

In the chapter "Spirit-Matter," the work of the patterning spirit in evolution is described more fully. It remains here to supply an argument for the connection of physical reality and spiritual reality which will be a bit more precise than that description.

The statements which we have seen defining the psychic in terms of the possibility of the application of will can help clarify the fact that spiritual reality, as defined here, is not psychic in itself. It clearly operates in evolution to organize matter prior to the advent of consciousness in any form, e.g., in the development of heavy elements out of hydrogen in stellar processes. Therefore, a connection between physical reality and spiritual reality must be a pre-psychic connection, i.e., a psychoid one. If spiritual reality were a brain process (as some philosophers would have it) it would *ipso facto* be connected with physical reality. But it is prior to brain and accounts for the existence of brain—in fact for all organism or organization. Thus all organization of matter is evidence for the connection of these two realities. If they seem distinct and even contradictory, still they *are* connected in perceptible forms. Beyond perceptibility also they are connected in the psychoid reality.

Beyond psychoid reality, if this expression has any possible meaning, we may make room in thought for an ultimate reality, the Source of all limitation, which is the same as saying the Source of all creation. And yet, if ultimate reality is not psychoid, it is wholly other than that of which it is the source, for the whole cosmos, spirit-matter, is psychoid in its potential for developing consciousness. We must also always keep in mind that ultimate reality, if its nature can be qualified at all, is just as much physical as spiritual. We may therefore search out the nature of God through the study of so-called matter just as effectively and necessarily as through the study of spirit.

BEING AND EXISTENCE

In order to clarify the present approach to the distinction between 'being' and 'existence,' we may look at three possible formulations:

1. *Existence* is physical reality, while *being* is spiritual reality.
2. The word *existence* applies to psychic reality, while *being* applies to the transpsychic realities—physical, spiritual, and archetypal.
3. The word *existence* describes physical and spiritual reality as well as psychic reality. Thus it applies to the world of multiplicity, leaving "being" as the predicate of archetypal reality and possibly of an ultimate reality, i.e., of a relatively undisturbed unity. An ultimate reality would have fewer properties or at least fewer *knowable* properties.

The first of these formulations would amount to a redundant renaming of the classes of reality involved, while the second would deny, as Kant did, the fact that knowledge corresponds quite objectively to that which is known. When we cross a street we can quite effectively trust our sense of sight to tell us whether or not we will be hit by a car. The third formulation can be shown, as will shortly be done, to correspond to the approaches to existence of Kierkegaard and of physics.

A fourth formulation expresses different aspects from those of the first three, yet demands to be correlated with them:

4. "Existence" is predicated of that which is particularized in space and time, whereas "being" describes that which is not so limited and which is yet subject to discussion.

Modern experiments, beginning with those of parapsychologist J. B. Rhine, have shown the capacity of the psychic realm, or the immediately transpsychic realms, for relativizing space and time, so care is needed with this foundation. If, however, with Jung and Jaffe, we see an archetypal reality as the source of this relativity, a close correspondence of the fourth formulation to the third is obtained.

Soren Kierkegaard, widely regarded as the father of Existentialism, approaches the difference between being and existence in terms of a transition between the two, i.e., "coming into existence" from a state of being. We will find that Kierkegaard, or S.K. as he is called in the literature, has meaningful parallels in physics, so that a discussion of what he has to say on the subject will aid our understanding of what "coming into existence" means physically.

The fact that Kierkegaard is concerned mainly with the eternal coming into time and especially with the eternal God becoming "the God in time" hardly reduces the generality of the material about to be quoted, if we see this as the problem of all creation, as Teilhard did. Moreover, the expression "the eternal coming into time," as will be seen, can well be applied to the physical discussion which follows on the transition from electromagnetic radiant energy to matter.

Kierkegaard says:

> In what sense is there change in that which comes into existence?... For if the subject of coming into existence does not itself remain unchanged during the change of coming into existence, it is not that which comes into existence, but something else...This coming-into-existence kind of change, therefore, is not a change in essence but in being, and is a transition from not-existing to existing. But this nonbeing which the subject of coming into existence leaves behind must itself have some sort of being...for every change always presupposes some thing which changes. (Kierkegaard, 1962, pp. 90-91).

S.K. then names these two forms of being "possibility" (the being prior to coming into existence) and "actuality" (that which exists in space and time). Possibility is not a nothing, but a something (one is tempted to say, an *actual* possibility), for it is grounded in the *necessary* and receives its *being* there:

> Can the necessary come into existence? Coming into existence is a change, but the necessary cannot be changed, since it always relates itself to itself and relates itself to itself in the same way. All coming into existence is a suffering, and the necessary cannot suffer; it cannot undergo the suffering of the actual, which is that the possible (not only the excluded possibility but also the accepted possibility) reveals itself as nothing in the moment it becomes actual. Everything which comes into existence proves precisely by coming into existence that it is not necessary, for the only thing which cannot come into existence is the necessary, because the necessary *is*. Is not necessity then a synthesis of possibility and actuality? What could this mean? Possibility and actuality do not differ in essence but in being; how could there from this difference be formed a synthesis constituting necessity, which is not a determination of being but a determination of essence, since it is the essence of the necessary to be. (Kierkegaard, 1962, pp. 91-92)

Here it is clear that the necessary confers *being* and participates in the change of coming into existence as that which does not change, and while it is the *essence* of that which comes into existence, it is also absolutely *other*:

> The necessary is a category entirely by itself. Nothing ever comes into existence with necessity; likewise the necessary never comes into existence and something by coming into existence never becomes the necessary. Nothing whatever exists

> because it is necessary or because the necessary is. The actual is not more necessary than the possible, for the necessary is absolutely different from both (Kierkegaard, 1962, pp. 91-92)

This "necessary" can thus be seen as related to the "ground of being" of Tillich and to "ultimate reality" in this book. "Possibility" is an intermediate level which is other than the necessary, for a possibility can be differentiated from other possibilities, but the actual is that which exists in space and time. As Nils Thulstrup says in the commentary to the work at hand: "Actuality is here understood as empirical, historical actuality." *(Ibid.*, p.238)

The definitions of physical and spiritual reality given above denote just such actualities in space and time. S.K. simply does not question the view which philosophers call "naive realism," i.e., belief that the outer world is just what it appears to be. Thus he lumps psychic, physical, and spiritual realities into one. If existence is actuality in space and time, and if things come into existence from the state of *being*, then being would be matched with archetypal reality. The word *archetype* precisely expresses possibilities for actualization.

In physics the model of the atomic nucleus now gaining much experimental support is the one in which the two relatively stable constituents of the nucleus—protons and neutron—are made up of "quarks" which are held together by "gluons." But quarks and gluons can never come into existence as single particles, even theoretically. They are therefore quite close to the nature of archetypes, which also are known only through their effects and never directly seen. This is one phenomenon which points to the level of being behind existence.

Several other physical indications of the distinction between being and existence will be seen in what follows. The tangible forms of matter (chemical elements) are derived by known stellar and cosmic processes from the two stable kinds of particles, protons and electrons. Thus, the problem of physical becoming can, to a first approximation at least, be subsumed under a discussion of the becoming of these two in relation to the acquisition of their simpler properties: mass, electrical charge, spin (pseudo-mechanical spin),[2] and the ability to come to rest in a space-time framework.

These two kinds of particles come into existence (in the early moments of the cosmos) by a well-known process called "pair production," which is reproducible in the laboratory. The antecedent state of a pair of particles is a single photon of sufficient mass for the manufacture either of a pair of electrons or a pair of protons.[3] This photon, on being disturbed, splits into two particles which have equal and opposite spin. Both of these particles can come to rest if physically separated from the other kind of particle (the kind created with it). If these opposite particles come together, they "annihilate" each

---

2. These first three are the properties which determine the physical properties of the 100-odd chemical elements. The chemical and macrophysical properties of these elements depend on the arrangement and interaction of the three properties in the *electrons* which are, in turn, arranged according to the nuclear properties of the atoms, i.e., the arrangement of protons (and of neutrons derived from the protons in the above-mentioned stellar processes) in the atomic nuclei.

3. The term *photon* applies to all electromagnetic radiation, from radio "waves," through microwaves, infrared, visible light, ultraviolet and x-rays, to gamma rays. In this case we have to do with gamma rays of great energy, i.e., of great mass.

other, returning to the photon state. Thus, in each pair, whether of electrons or protons, one particle is called "matter" and the other "antimatter."

Let us call the photon state "being," for it lacks some of the properties of "existence," and by examining these properties let us see how accurate an analogy we have constructed.

First, in "mass" we have a property corresponding to S.K.'s "that which remains the same in coming into existence": we observe the rigorous conservation of mass in the pair-production process. Here we use Einstein's $E = mc^2$ to equate mass with energy. Photons have weight and are attracted by gravitating bodies, including other photons.

Secondly, in the properties of electrical charge and of spin, we have examples of the coming into existence of *new* properties by means of opposites, whereby there is no *net* increase of charge or of spin. At the same time, from our standpoint of hindsight, we can see how these actualities were present as *possibilities* in the photon, especially as regards electric charge, for the electromagnetic fields which constitute the photon are the same as those produced by such charges once those charges *exist*.

Lastly, the property of being capable of rest points to existence as *being there*, i.e., in space and time. In fact, only *such* particles, and *not* photons, can be used to define space and time as such. As to this property of rest not being applicable to photons, we refer to Einstein's Relativity (as verified by experiment) where it is known that for particles traveling at the speed of photons, *no time passes*. A photon has *no duration* in its own framework and therefore *all distances* in the photon's framework are the same, namely zero. Therefore such a framework cannot be used to define either space or time. Yet we *do* construct frameworks of space and time, based on matter particles, in which photons *are seen as* traveling from one definite point to another and as taking finite times to do so. This paradox separates the real *being* of photons from the real *existence* of matter, but being and existence remain related and undergo interactions mutually.

Matter-antimatter pairs of particles arise (cosmically) within a self-related[4] aggregation of photons because they are part of the possibility of *being* of this aggregation. With the additional properties and limitations just discussed, *existence* arises in its clearly dual character. Something physically eternal has thus become limited and subject to time and space.

Along with the possibilities *for* matter, we must examine the possibilities for its modes of development —the complexities of its possible interactions. This, we know, is not determined particle by particle but is *patterned,* as we will see. Jung's use of the term *archetype* as pattern, not only of spirit but of physical world as well, fits our need admirably, though the preceding discussion of photons exemplifies only a small and relatively simple portion of archetypal reality. The "quarks" and "gluons" mentioned earlier give another aspect, but still a very primitive one. Human archetypes are infinitely more complex, though they still partake of both spirit and matter. In Chapter Six we will see how these human archetypes may have arisen by complexification from the much simpler situation pictured here.

In summary, we may say that existence is *limited*

---

4. These words are consciously chosen to recall the quotation from Soren Kierkegaard, above, and also the opening of his *The Sickness Unto Death* (Walter Lowrie, trans., Princeton: Princeton Univ. Press, 1954). The words apply to the aggregate under discussion as a "sphere whose center is everywhere and whose circumference is nowhere," as discussed in Chapter Three.

being, the primary limitations being those of space and time, and that form of duality is known as complementarity. Thus existence includes psychic reality, physical reality, and spiritual reality, but not archetypal reality or the ultimate reality behind the archetypal. The word *being* applies to archetypal and ultimate reality.

PHENOMENOLOGICAL GROUNDING OF REALITY

In including the three realities, psychic, physical, and spiritual, within existence, it becomes possible to clarify what the word *phenomenon* might mean, for generally its meaning is different for philosophers from what it is for physicists. In Chapter Four we will also see that fine distinctions in the meaning of *phenomenon* are crucial to the differing world-views of physicists.

In philosophical phenomenology, the word *phenomenon* usually refers to a *mental* event since our experience is mental or psychic. In physics, on the other hand, the term refers to events in an assumed outer world, though still retaining the connotation of events *as perceived*. However, an "outer world" has much less philosophical certainty than does the mental realm.

In what follows the distinction between the physical and the psychic will be clarified, along with the problem involved in making the distinction. As in the previous section, many well-known problems are avoided by the acceptance of the essential role of the observer.

Each event which purports to convey experience of an outside world is, as experienced, a representation of an image to the ego, i.e., it is a *psychic* event. Philosophers know well the difficulty of establishing the certainty of anything other than such psychic phenomena. We all tend to agree that it is as if there were an outside world, but we find it impossible to draw unequivocal evidence of the physical because the ego, being psychic, can experience directly only the psychic and not the physical.

In the definitions of various kinds of reality just given, physical reality was defined as containing certain kinds of experience of limitation, which are, in the main, quite distinct, *as experienced*, from other kinds of limitations. In this sense it is not necessary to solve the problem which is put in the paragraph above, for all phenomena then remain psychic phenomena, including those which, because of their distinction in quality from spiritual-rational phenomena, we call physical.

Still, if we left the matter there, we would not be doing justice to the *kind* of independence, i.e., objectivity, which is characteristic of the "outer world" in its relation to the ego and which demands that a description other than psychic at least be included. Since the psychic is closely associated with *will*, the need for this distinction is even clearer: we do not typically speak of the will of inanimate objects.

Moreover, we would be left with another disturbing paradox. Assuming that there is an outer world, we have accounted in detail for physical stimuli acting on the human body (which is a part of this outer world), and we can follow the physiological transmission of nerve impulses to the brain. Now, what is to be the solution of the problem of how these impulses become psychic representations to the ego?

The question itself implies a distinction in kind between the physical and the psychic, and this is fine because we assumed the physical as distinct to begin with. But what if we don't make that assumption? The question remains; the problem is now formulated within the psychic realm, but the radical difference between what is now the quasiphysical psychic and the quasipsychic psychic is not abrogated. The distinction is just as compelling as before and Occam's razor demands that we cut off the complexification of "quasi" and the redundant "psychic" in the formulation just given. We say "just as compelling" since in neither case is it *absolutely* compelling, nor can it be, for in the end we must admit again that the ego cannot experience the physical immediately, and thus we cannot *know* it with certainty.

Given the radical distinction between the physical and the psychic, which holds in any case, the problem arises as to how accurate the psychic image is with respect to the physical reality. In the frontier regions of physics, the microphysical and cosmological realms, we have learned that even highly successful images or models may be radically wrong. In the middle realm of macrophysical events, on the other hand, the images normally seem to be highly differentiated and highly reliable.[5]

Figure 1 is a diagram or flow chart which summarizes those realms of physical reality which are essential for the discussions to follow in the later chapters, and which indicates the possible meanings of the word *phenomenon*.

As used in this book, *phenomenon* refers primarily to events in the macroscopic "middle realm" of this outer world, which is designated level 2 of physical

---

5. A strong argument for "naive realism" which is overlooked by many philosophers is the fact that each of us is a *public* observer of the "outer world," not a private one. My two eyes see different views of the outer world, and these views are correlated to a third: that provided by touch. The other senses provide secondary corroboration.

reality in the diagram. As noted above, this is the realm of the greatest reliability of our concepts as applicable to the world. It is often noted that Einstein did not change the *facts known to Newton, but our understanding* of those facts. This indicates the stability and reliability of this middle realm. Moreover, all microphysical events are transmitted to the ego via the macrophysical, whence we speak of "phenomenon," "perceived phenomenon," and "apperceived phenomenon,"[6] referring to the following three levels: microphysical-macrophysical event, macrophysical impingement of the event on the senses, and ego-acceptance of the image of the event.

Phenomenology is the study and description of these events in communicable (primarily rational) terms, which includes reflection upon the events and the application to them of such categories as can be agreed upon.

Phenomenological grounding will be taken to mean that, in securing the above-mentioned agreement, *phenomena*, or as physicists call them, *observables*, can be only final arbiters. This is not to claim that there is a pure phenomenon absolutely apart from theory or concept but that experimental considerations take precedence over purely theoretical ones such as symmetry, simplicity, and elegance. Thus, we admit that: (1) our concepts are only partial; (2) phenomena have, as in the case of Einstein's relativity theory, forced the regrounding of whole branches of physics and philosophy; and (3) as just discussed, we have only psychic images of the "outer world," not direct knowledge. After all, physical laws as we know them are not what govern the universe but merely our attempts to *describe* that which does.

---

6. Apperception is described in the next chapter.

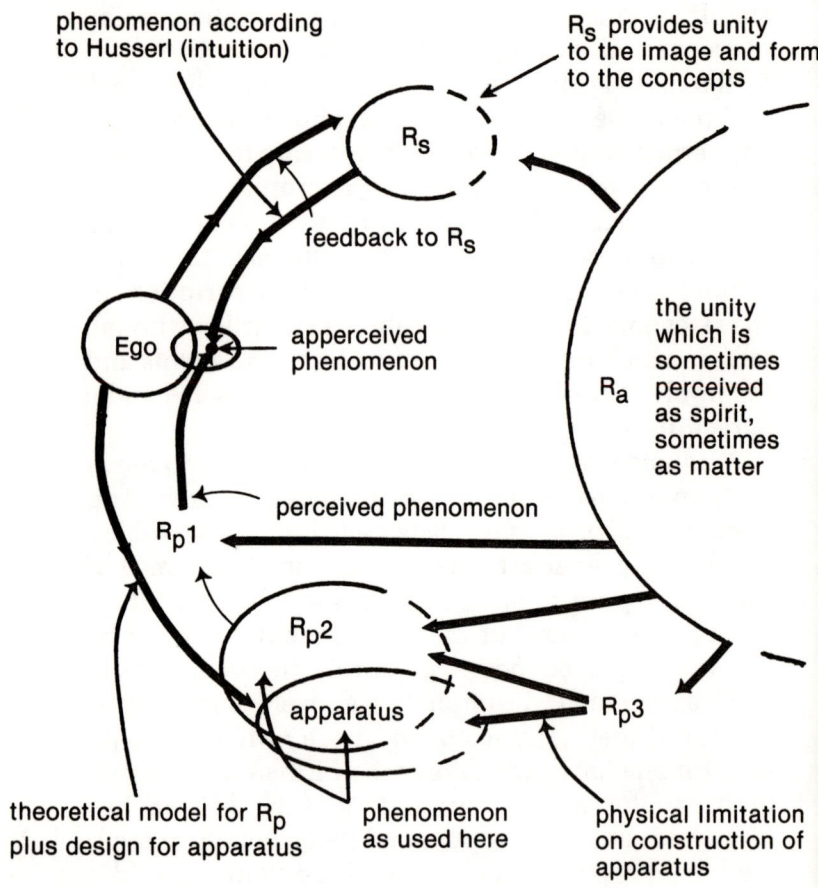

Figure 1. The Ego and Levels of Reality

Comments

(1) General: In the definition of "reality," physical reality was divided into three, namely, the physiological, the macroscopic, and the microscopic (referring to atomic and nuclear dimensions). Here these three are labeled R_{p1}, R_{p2}, and R_{p3}, respectively. "Memory" and phenomena of conscious reflection are not placed on the diagram. It is known at least that learning alters brain structure so that there is some physiological component to these.

(2) R_s (spiritual reality): Implicit in this schema is the notion that the contents of R_s, like those of R_p, must be *transformed* into psychic images in order to be brought into relation to the ego. We do not know the *mechanism* of the development of R_s evolutionarily, but assume that it is closely related to the known sequence of the development of concepts from emotions.

(3) R_a (archetypal reality): It is because of the unity of "spirit-matter" that R_a assures that R_s will *correspond* to R_p in the apperceived phenomenon. We may also argue the connection of R_s with R_p as follows: R_s is not psychic in itself because it operated before consciousness. Therefore a connection must be a prepsychic connection. Now, if R_s were a brain process, it would be *ipso facto* connected with R_p, a fact apparently overlooked by those who, like Einstein, make the Kantian assumption. But R_s is prior to brain, and accounts for the existence of brain. That is, the existence of brain (here used as representative of all organism) is taken as evidence of the said connection of R_s and R_p.

(4) R_{p2} (level of human experience): We discover and learn language, and thus rational categories, as macroscopic facts. Specific languages, in which all philosophy is "done," are sustained only "out there" in specific cultures, whence each individual derives them. But language never relinquishes its archetypal connection to R_s and is never wholly rational. The direct line from R_{p3} to R_{p2} refers to the fact that the stability of matter is due to "quantum" effects, as was brought out in the last chapter. The relationships in this diagram will be greatly elaborated by means of another diagram in Chapter Three.

One reason for placing a definition of phenomenology in this chapter is to dissociate the word as used in this book from its usual philosophical connotations, and particularly its association with Edmund Husserl and the philosophical schools which have branched out from his. For Husserl, the object of the *cogito* (of Descartes) is the *cogitatum*. If we meditate on any "physical" thing, what consciousness does is to examine those pure "intelligibles" or intelligible ideas which are "given" *through* the thing, not the sense impression itself. Thus, for Husserl, the *phenomenon* is the *pure* phenomenon (in the Kantian sense), that which is purely "intelligible," stripped of all which might be contingent. That is, the mind deals not with an external object but with ideas representing what seems to be an object; the mind deals only with *thought*. Husserl, like Kant, falls into the trap of calling these phenomena "a priori," "eternal," and "absolute."[7]

Central in the problems involved with phenomenology, and especially in the definition of *phenomenon*, is the notion of the nature of the *a priori* function in the psyche. We may cite as early a work as Aristotle's Physics for a principle whose validity is only now being challenged: gross experience can be analyzed to arrive at that which is necessarily true and clear *in itself*. Descartes also had the impression that the rational mind held and used that which was "clear and distinct" as the agent of its *a priori* functioning, but it was Kant who put the matter in its starkest terms:

> We shall understand by a priori knowledge, not knowledge independent of this or that experience,

---

7. Lauer, 1965, pp. 15-16, 30-32.

but knowledge absolutely independent of all experience. (Kant, 1965, p. 43)

Kant also used the terms "absolute necessity" and "absolute universality" as properties of pure *a priori* propositions, judgments, and categories. However, the criteria of clarity, universality and necessity simply are no longer tenable in themselves. But aside from everything which Kant described as absolute, the basic reason that the *a priori* function cannot have absolute contents is that it has evolved over the aeons as a function of the *experience* of protoplasm in the process of development.

Husserl also labors under an essentially 19th century notion of mathematics, namely that: "Mathematical essences are static and changeless; they can be fixed once and for all and described with perfect exactitude." (Lauer, 1965, p. 18) Two years after Husserl retired, mathematician Kurt Gödel proved that this is an untenable position. The comment attached to the above diagram, relating to the fact that concepts rest upon emotions, indicates another reason why even mathematics may not claim absolute certainty: it rests on concepts and thus, ultimately, on the contingent. Jung comments on this point as follows:

> The moment one forms an idea of a thing and successfully catches one of its aspects, one invariably succumbs to the illusion of having caught the whole. One never considers that a total apprehension is right out of the question. Not even an idea posited as total is total, for it is still an entity on its own with unpredictable qualities. This self-deception certainly promotes peace of mind: the unknown is named, the far has been brought near, so that one can lay one's finger on it. One has taken possession of it, and it has become an in-

alienable piece of property, like a slain creature of the wild that can no longer run away. It is a magical procedure such as the primitive practices upon objects and the psychologist upon the psyche. He is no longer at its mercy, but he never suspects that the very fact of grasping the object conceptually gives it a golden opportunity to display all those qualities which would never have made their appearance had it not been imprisoned in a concept. (Jung, 1969c, p. 168)

Jung's view of phenomenology can be given rather compactly in his own words:

I am an empiricist and adhere as such to the phenomenological standpoint...I believe that experience is not even possible without reflection, because 'experience is a process of assimilation without which there could be no understanding.'...This standpoint is exclusively phenomenological, that is, it is concerned with occurrences, events, experiences...in a word, with facts. Its truth is a fact and not a judgment. When psychology speaks, for instance, of the motif of the virgin birth, it is only concerned with the fact that there is such an idea, but it is not concerned with the question whether such an idea is true or false in any other sense. The idea is psychologically true inasmuch as it exists...[Likewise] an elephant is 'true' because it exists. The elephant is neither an inference nor a statement nor the subjective judgment of a creator. It is a phenomenon. (Jung, 1969b, pp. 5-7)

Here it is clear that the macroscopic outer world (R_{p2} in Figure 1) is the locus of phenomena. It is also clear that Jung's view coincides with that of the definition given above. In all of his works Jung stresses what he calls his *empiricism*, which is the same as that which has here been called "phenomenological grounding," as distinct, again, from philosophical schools which are called "empiricist."

3
The Way of Knowing

Who knows in truth? Who can tell us whence and how arose this universe? The gods are later than its beginning: who knows therefore whence comes this creation?

Only that god who sees in highest heaven; he only knows whence comes this universe, and whether it was made or uncreated. He only knows, or perhaps he knows not.

Rig Veda X, 129

When we use the question Who knows? we are not ordinarily looking for an answer but intend to terminate the conversation, or at least the subject at hand. Sometimes we use the alternative expression "God only knows" for the same purpose. When Erhard Scheibe wrote, "Knowledge known to none is no knowledge," he evidently had physicists in mind and not God. Yet if we follow the example of the physicists themselves, it is not irrelevant to bring God into the discussion. Einstein's famous statement shows this:

> I can believe that God governs the world in any manner you may care to specify, but I refuse to believe that He plays at dice with the universe.

In other words, God knows.

What can *we* know and how can we know it? The ancient philosophers were in general agreement that we can know the nature of things best by means of our pure rationality; that the world of observable phenomena is very deceptive. Martin Schwarzschild expressed this idea when he said (Chapter Two) that pure thought should be capable of discovering the laws which govern the universe. Einstein agreed not only that this way of knowing is possible for physics, but went further to assert that this is in fact how physics is done. In *The World as I See It* (1935), he asserted that fundamental physical laws are "free inventions of the human intellect." More recently, physicists have been trying to find what they pre-judicially call a "ghost-free [observerless] axiomatization" of quantum physics. The point of view of this book is that such endeavors are impossible to fulfill. This being so, it is necessary to present the case for the position taken.

The heart of this chapter will be a diagram show-ing the relationship of ego-consciousness to both matter and spirit. Earlier, this same topic was ap-proached from several angles. These are not neces-sarily independent points.

1. Ego-consciousness is related to both the matter and spirit aspects of that which is unconscious by means of the guiding fact that ego-consciousness has evolved from spirit-matter.

2. All of our knowledge is psychic in nature and must be mediated from the nonpsychic (trans-psychic) realities of spirit and matter. Psyche perceives that such is the case and *feels* both the separation-from and belonging-to a transpsychic reality. The psychic nature of knowledge applies even to the so-called laws of physics which are only our attempts to *describe* that which governs the universe. It is wrong in principle to say that the laws of physics *govern* the universe.

3. The fact that we begin in the middle is essentially the same fact stated in the previous two points. It is bolstered by the fact that sciences cannot establish permanent foundations. Physical facts remain, but the foundations may be as diverse as those of Newton and Einstein.

In this chapter, we will add more aspects:

4. Philosophy has demonstrated that we cannot know the thing-in-itself, that all our knowledge is distorted and yet must spring somehow from the object.
5. Religion and science are ways of knowing, and knowing implies a knower. The ultimate way of knowing is through observation which necessarily disturbs that which is being observed. But this, too, is a form of relationship of the ego with both spirit and matter.

In later chapters the fourth point will be expanded as it relates to physics. It is impossible even to define the word *phenomenon* apart from the conceptual framework used by observers, for the measuring equipment of physicists is designed with concepts in mind as to what is to be observed and how to go about it.

As will be shown in this chapter, the very conceptual framework has developed out of experience, in a very broad sense, including the whole scope of evolution over billions of years. More particularly, the development of the ego in modern individuals follows this whole evolutionary process. The ego's relation to both spirit and matter will be shown from the similarity of the models which have been used as symbols of totality in both realms.

The nature of the relationship was first suggested by the applicability of a particular model both to the "self" as the center and totality of the human psyche and to the physical cosmos as well. This model is the "finite circle [or sphere] whose center is everywhere and whose circumference is nowhere." This phrase is nonrational, but nonetheless it *does* apply with mathematical rigor to the best current model of the physical universe.

The idea behind this model comes from Parmenides, if not earlier, and has been employed by Plato and Christian gnostics, mystics, and alchemists over the millenia (Jung, 1969b, p. 155). Jung associates it with the mandala in general as a God-image of the Self, among other god images.[1]

Besides making use of this model of the God-circle, the diagram is grounded in the guiding fact of the evolutionary development of ego-consciousness out of that which is unconscious. In particular, this evolution implies not only that spirit, matter, and psyche are aspects of one reality, but also that our

---

1. Jung also refers to a complementary image found in the apocryphal *Acts of John:* For your sakes this cross of light was named by me now Logos, now Nous, now Jesus, now Christ, now Door, now Way, now Bread, now Seed, now Resurrection, now Son, now Father, now Grace. So it is called for men; but in itself and in its essence, as spoken of to you, it is the Boundary of all things, and the composing of things unstable, and the harmony of wisdom, and the wisdom that is in harmony. (*Ibid.*, p 282.)

Of the image, Jung says:

> The definition of the cross or center as the 'boundary of all things' is exceedingly original, for it suggests that the limits of the universe are not to be found in a nonexistent periphery but in its center. There alone resides the possibility of transcending this world. All instability culminates in that which is unchanging and quiescent, and in the self all disharmonies are resolved in the 'harmony of wisdom.' (p. 285)

The image is complementary, for it refers to the cross rather than to the circle (Jung, 1969b, pp. 155f).

concepts are of nonrational origin. Therefore we must deal with two so-called ideals of science: objectivity or detachment and absolute conceptual clarity. After doing so, we can then present the diagram.

Objectivity is a rather paradoxical concept. In an absolute sense it would imply that ego-consciousness is absolutely detached from matter, but this detachment simply is not the case. The relation of the ego to the world is one both of *disconnection* from the world and *connection* to the world. The disconnection is best considered as a condition arising evolutionarily *out of connection* with, or groundedness in, the world. In a variety of senses, this process is "against nature," but it really is a compensatory process within nature, balancing unconscious "nature," with consciousness. The connection is founded on a fundamental *disconnection*, the fact that the perceived world is not the world-in-itself. Nonetheless, something is perceived which is both outer and not-I. Let us look at these two relationships. The separation will be considered first, then the inclusion.

The disconnection of "I" from "world" is partly grounded in the disconnection of the ego from the inner "not-I." We will see later that the inner "not-I" mediates the perception of the outer "not-I" by the ego. Therefore we need not make a strong distinction between the inner and outer "world," but can focus on the ego in its separation from both.

Two basic lines of evidence allow us to detail the evolution of ego-consciousness out of the unconscious: the content of myths and the development of consciousness within the individual during life. These two are parallel to each other.

Of his book *The Origin and History of Consciousness*, Erich Neumann says:

It is the task of this book to show that a series of archetypes is a main constituent of mythology, that they stand in an organic relation to one another, and that their succession as stages of development determines the growth of consciousness. In the course of its ontogenetic development, the individual ego consciousness has to pass through the same archetypal stages which determined the evolution of consciousness in the life of humanity.

The mythological stages in the evolution of consciousness begin with the stage when the ego is contained in the unconscious and lead up to a situation in which the ego not only becomes aware of its own position and defends it heroically but also becomes capable of broadening and relativizing its experiences through the changes effected by its own activity. (Neumann, 1954, pp. xvi, 5)

These claims are not self-evident—Neumann devotes 450 pages to the "task" of demonstrating them. Jung also has numerous references to the parallelism.[2] The purpose of bringing the *conclusion* here is to justify concentrating on the development of the individual ego alone, rather than taking up both lines of evidence now. We will let Neumann's study carry the burden of the mythic line. The discussion of the "ontogenetic development" of the ego-complex primarily will follow Jung's essay, "The Stages of Life" (in 1969c).

The ego is not present at birth. The evidence from recognition, memory, and the like is that the first development is of "islands of consciousness" which are gradually connected, perhaps like an "arche-

---

2. See, for example, *The Structure and Dynamics of the Psyche*, (1969c), pp. 152, 158, and *Psychology and Religion* (1969b), pp. 289-291, 490.

pelago." Moreover, these "islands" only gradually acquire subjective value:

> This series...is at first merely perceived, and for this reason the child logically begins by speaking of itself objectively in the third person. Only later, when the ego-contents—the so-called ego-complex—have acquired an energy of their own (very likely as a result of training and practice) does the feeling of subjectivity of "I-ness" arise (Jung, 1969c, p. 390).

Jung stresses the role of *problems* in the development of the ego's continuity and strength. For the infant there are no true problems requiring cogitation and decision. Here, simple conflict and lack of immediate satisfaction serve the still simple process of differentiation, but there is no ambivalence. The latter is characteristic of consciousness where a trust in instinct and a trust in rational decision are both fearful and dubious paths.

> The biblical fall of man presents the dawn of consciousness as a curse. And as a matter of fact it is in this light that we first look on every problem that forces us to greater consciousness and separates us even further from the paradise of unconditioned childhood. (Jung, 1969c, pp. 388f)

In general, the crises of adolescence—if encountered—produce a continuity of subjectivity. These are genuine *inner* crises of ambivalence about one's "identity" and even about one's lack of outer problems, if such is the case.

In one sense the discussion of disconnection is complete with the establishing of the "I"—subject and object are distinct. But this stage is characterized by a false connection of another kind: the sense of possessiveness that makes the lover say, "That is *my* woman," the bank teller say, "That is *my* bank," the poet say, "That is *my* poem." None of these are "objective" statements; all indicate an incomplete personality. This postadolescent stage is also characterized by a false disconnection from the world. As Jung says:

> The development of modern consciousness so far has made it emancipated enough to forget its dependence on the unconscious psyche. It is not a little proud of this emancipation, but it overlooks the fact that although it has apparently got rid of the unconscious it has become the victim of its own verbal concepts...Man's advance towards the Logos was a great achievement, but he must pay for it with loss of instinct and loss of reality to the degree that he remains in primitive dependence on mere words. (Jung, 1969b, p. 290)

The attitude described is typical of the postadolescent and the sense of having "come of age." That this represents a false state, a state of repressed problems, is shown empirically by consideration of the crises of middle life which occur when the loss of meaning becomes unbearable. This occurs with far fewer persons than the crises of adolescence. Most of us are largely content with "I-awareness" and with letting significant inner and outer events pass us by or else happen to us as suits them, rather than taking on the work of active relationship to them.

This suggests that part of the solution to the crisis of meaning, the next stage in the development of consciousness, is what might be called "being present" to both outer and inner worlds. Being "present" to something is an opening of the soul to that something, or bringing the whole person to whatever is the essence of the moment. This is a rather rare phenomenon because of the courage and religious awareness which it requires. For most of us it can best be described as not blocking out our awareness of either the darkest or the highest sides of our nature. We also use cultural images to block our awareness of all of the possibilities in a given situation. We know of those rare humans who can really *be* with others, usually because they have encompassed much suffering. The eminent black theologian, Howard Thurman, told of being called to the bedside of a man whose condition was so desperate that Thurman could not find the words. He said, "I took his hand, and together we stormed the gates of heaven for an hour, though neither of us spoke." Afterward, the man thanked Thurman deeply. Something had happened, because Thurman was able to be fully present, though nonverbally.

The need for courage is the need for what Tillich calls the "courage to be": to face the fact of the human situation with its alienations and darknesses and unacceptability, and the real interdependence of I and not-I. Where the decision is made to face these facts, "being present" can develop, as did I-awareness, first as islands, then as a continent. This is the true religion, the reconnection of that which has been split apart—the split, as Tillich says, occurring and being sustained as "fate" and as "guilt."

Thus, the subjective sense of independence represents only a partial truth. Nonetheless, the ego is quite correctly called a subject, receiving images, knowledge, and communication from a relatively objective outer world. Still, we must keep in mind, as already pointed out, that, as Jung put it:

> The only form of existence of which we have immediate knowledge is psychic. We might well say, on the contrary, that physical existence is a mere inference, since we know of matter only insofar as

we perceive psychic images mediated by the
senses. (Jung, 1969b, p. 12)

The ego is bombarded with images, not all of
which come to conscious awareness. Those that do
are said not only to be perceived but apperceived.
Apperception naturally has degrees, both as to what
is selected from the field of perceived images, ideas,
and memories, and as to the impact it has on
awareness. We receive more easily into awareness
those contents which are most like what we already
know. The optimum quality of apperception is well
described by the word *articulated* as it is used with
respect to the bones in our fingers: flexibly, adjusted-
ly, jointedly connected to what is already there, i.e.,
to the existing contents of the ego.[3] We also say that
an apperceived idea is *clear* when one takes a second
step of articulating the idea or content with words in
a meaningful way. All understanding amounts to
becoming *accustomed* to whatever is understood.
Such, then, is how a psychic content such as an im-

---

3. A good model for articulation, which is both an inner and
outer model, is the life process of a nuclear body cell: all of the
possibilities are present as a simple structure in the DNA. ("Simple" here refers to the fact that basically a four-letter "alphabet"
of molecules is strung together into the "words" which contain
the information as to how to make the proteins which a cell
makes. The "grammatical" rules also are simple.) It is the great
length of the sentence and its words, the length of which follows
upon, and is symbolic of, the evolutionary process, which gives
the human "given" its complexity. "Images" are sent as shorter
RNA from the nucleus to the "ribosomes" in the cell where they
attract the needed components and *articulate* them into "words,"
which words are the proteins which perform so many life functions in the body. The word *archetype* applies quite literally to
the RNA, and the analogue elucidates Jung's use of the word as
well. The archetype (RNA) is behind the concrete identifiable
part of the archetype which contains the totality of the RNA patterns, namely the nuclear DNA.

age of a part of the outer or inner world becomes related to the ego, i.e., becomes conscious.

A helpful example, frequently encountered, is the sense of God-presence in nature. A perceived image of an object, event, or process, whether simple or complex, from the outer world may serve as a "gate" by providing the model for the articulation of a previously unapperceived inner image in which great energy is stored. The apperception, happening with the articulation of the image from outside, combined with the energy and affect from within, endows the "object" with numinosity, with otherness. Two famous examples of this are noted in the lives of Brother Lawrence and Jacob Boehme, whose visions were opened and mediated by a tree in winter and a metal cup, respectively.

The important point for the model of the psyche being presented is that the numinosity is not part of the *response* of the I, though it is in the person; it is part of the *stimulus*, it is not-I. Though it is "other" to the ego, it is part of the *sameness* of the inner and outer worlds which have evolved together.

Moreover, this sameness of the dual not-I realms is the ground of *all* learning, for energy from the archetypal realm of *meaning* must accompany any image which is to be received as value and thus retained by ego-consciousness. That is to say, all learning is experience of meaning, though not all learning is of the intensity of "religious experience" in the more common usage of the term.

At the same time, the ego-complex must bear *some* relationship of similarity to *both* inner and outer not-I realms, for it is evolutionarily grounded in, or rests upon, a dual transpsychic basis, matter and spirit. Only such a similarity could make experience or apperception of the not-I possible. This second dimension of similarity is the subject of the next paragraphs.

Immanuel Kant has had great influence on physicists, philosophers, and theologians. He argued cogently that the mind is active in perception and apperception, and for the unknowability of the "thing-in-itself" *(Ding-an-sich)*. What we know or perceive is only what our own intuitive and rational faculties give us to see in response to stimuli from outside. The stimuli themselves remain unknown. Kant's whole *Critique of Pure Reason* is an attempt to answer the question of how our concepts do apply to the outer world nonetheless!

Physicist Victor Lenzen, in an article which Einstein found "entirely convincing and correct," describes Einstein's attitude toward this problem:

> According to Einstein, the concepts which arise in thought and in our linguistic expressions logically are free creations of thought which cannot be derived from sensory experiences. Like Plato, Einstein stresses the gap between data of sense and concepts of thought. He contends that there is a gulf, logically unbridgeable, which separates the world of sensory experiences from the realm of concepts and conceptual relations which constitute propositions... Accordingly he asserts, 'In a certain sense, therefore, I hold it to be true that pure thought is competent to comprehend the real, as the ancients dreamed.' (Lenzen, 1949, pp. 380f)

The split between thought and world is often spoken of as that which is "given"—*a priori*, prior to experience and also prior to the jumbles of nerve impulses which our senses send to the brain—versus that which is derived from sensory experience—*a posteriori*. Both of these Latin terms are adverbial phrases.

A priori is a term originally applied to that which was thought of as truly independent of all experience, derived from intuitive truth, and true in itself because clear, distinct, and convincing. It also has connotations of causality, for that which is derived deductively from that which is already considered true *a priori* carries truth-value equal to that from which it is derived.

A priori intuitive truth is also considered the cause and basis of experience. These views held from Aristotle through Kant, who stated them in extremely strong terms:

> ...[I]t is possible to show that pure *a priori* principles are indispensable for the possibility of experience, and so prove their existence *a priori*. For whence could experience derive its certainty, if all the rules according to which it proceeds were always themselves empirical and therefore contingent? Such rules could hardly be regarded as first principles...Such *a priori* origin is manifest in certain concepts, no less than in judgments. If we remove from our empirical concept of a body, one by one, every feature in it which is merely empirical, the color, (etc.), there still remains the space which the body occupied, and this cannot be removed. Again, if we remove from our empirical concept of any object, corporeal or incorporeal, all properties which experience has taught us, we yet cannot take away that property through which that object is thought as substance or as inhering in a substance...Owing, therefore, to the necessity with which this concept of substance forces itself upon us, we have no option save to admit that it has its seat in our faculty of *a priori* knowledge. (Kant, 1965, p. 45)

From a modern physical viewpoint, of course, this is so full of holes that it is difficult to imagine what Kant had in mind. Statistical mechanics, for instance, demonstrates that empirically derived certainty quite accounts for the consistencies of experience to which Kant must be referring. Moreover, the removal of properties is simply impossible mentally, to say nothing of physically, and in modern physics a concept of substance as a basis of some sort of inherence is simply unnecessary. The corrective for his position will be developed in the two sections to follow.

A *posteriori* denotes that which is derived from experience and carries a sense of particularity as opposed to generality or universality. What one derives from experience is always this or that particular thing. Where, then, do we get general principles? We notice regularities, but is the concept of regularity obtained *a priori* or *a posteriori*? Kant says that regularity is a general principle *a priori*, and Einstein similarly says, for example, that "the laws of physics are free inventions of the human intellect." But if we are to proceed, as all science does, from particulars to generalities, we must, in the main, proceed inductively.

In the quotation in Chapter Two in which Martin Schwarzschild asks whether or not "pure thought" should be able to uncover the "simple perfect laws" which he assumes govern the universe, we again have Kantian presuppositions: "simple and perfect" and "pure thought." Of course we do experience simplicity and a degree of completeness and there is much which can be discovered prior to observation, depending on how we have developed up to the time in question. In these matters, however, we inevitably deal in approximation. In fact, "laws" do not rule the universe at all, but are attempts to describe that which does. They are symbolic-mythic statements of an "as if" variety.

First of all, concepts as organizations of mental or visual images are phenomena of consciousness. As I see it, the correct evolutionary sequence, given the development of visual images as a synthesis of sense data in the brain, is (1) emotion, (2) image, (3) language, (4) concept, and (5) generalization, as can be seen from what follows, based primarily on the work of Jung.

In this scheme a clear concept is the peak of a pyramid whose base is nonrational experience, parallel to the development of consciousness out of the unconscious. This is the reverse of the "unpacking" theory (see Chapter 3), but it follows if one agrees that *language is prior to concepts*. In Jung's view:

> The material with which we think is *language* and *verbal concepts*—something which from time immemorial has been directed outwards and used as a bridge, and which has but a single purpose, namely that of communication...Language was originally a system of emotive and imitative sounds—sounds which express terror, fear, anger, love, etc., and sounds which imitate the noises of the elements...A large number of onomatopoeic vestiges remain even in the more modern languages...Thus language, in its origin and essence, is simply a system of signs or symbols that denote real occurrences or their echo in the human soul. (Jung, 1956, p. 12)

That is to say, Jung's theory holds that language begins essentially as *body* language, even if it is vocal. We tend to think of the times when we "knew what we wanted to say, but couldn't find the words" as indicating that the concept was prior to the language. But that is an artifact of our present state of development. If we imagine the "language" of simpler animals and work our way through the evolutionary scale, it should be evident that stimulus-response communication comes first, and that even our most abstract and spiritual thought can be traced in its origin to such simple things as making and breaking connections, or getting wounded and healing. In this scheme, *naming things* is already a high degree of abstraction, which occurred long after communication *about* things or situations.

The situation in physics in which the so-called first principles are so much more susceptible to fundamental change than are observations and observational principles is explained by these facts. Philosopher of science Michael Scriven said, "Physics has done very well without any foundations."

Conscious and unconscious, as they become differentiated *in human evolution*, represent the mutual development of opposites.

> Between "I do this" and "I am conscious of doing this" there is a world of difference, amounting sometimes to outright contradiction. Consequently there is a consciousness in which unconsciousness predominates, as well as a consciousness in which self-consciousness predominates. This paradox becomes immediately intelligible when we realize that there is no conscious content which can with absolute certainty be said to be totally conscious, for that would necessitate an unimaginable totality of consciousness... Jung, 1969c, p. 188)

We would like to deal with fundamental categories as if everyone easily understands them. However, they have a very complex developmental history. To name examples such as spirit, life, same, other, unity, matter, energy, thought, knowledge, motion, cause, and rationality is to list the battlefields in a bloody search for clear and distinct concepts—battlefields on which the struggle still continues as it has for millennia: "The history of thought has not dealt kindly with the doctrine of clear and distinct ideas" (Nagel, 1958, p. 23).

This fact, in itself, is enough with which to attack Kant's notion of the absolute and necessary character of the *a priori*. While it is true that without approximately fundamental and rational categories we cannot apperceive anything, it is also clear that these categories are not given, as the human is not given, but have evolved over the aeons as humanity has: they are concepts in a language that have been abstracted from concrete experiences.

We might use *particle* as an example and note that concepts like inertness versus fieldcenter, divisibility versus indivisibility (under varying circumstances), definiteness versus indefiniteness, and even the interchange of particle qualities for those of "wave" must be considered in precisely the microscopic physical realm where we would suppose the term *particle* to receive its most fundamental *definition*.

It might be objected that one nonetheless has a clear and distinct *notion* of "particle." Even Kant, however, insisted that the proper application of fundamental and rational categories is to the phenomena, but we now know that the *clear* category is a "null set," a category without examples, though as an approximate description, it applies to a great many phenomena. For example, if we were to try to define a category such as "Democrat" or "Republican," we might start with all persons who are registered as such. But we know that many people switch parties to vote against a candidate. And take those who consider themselves *predominantly* one or the other, and who register on that basis. What *is* a Democrat or Republican? As we try to sharpen the definition and assure the conformity of the candidates to that definition, the numbers diminish! Can I, the "true believer" in one or the other party, even be certain of myself beyond challenge? And so we generally find some quality which ought to fall within the category but which is lacking in any given candidate for inclusion. It is easy to set up categories and find lots of examples, but the process of clarification is impossible because clarification excludes candidates, and *ultimate* clarification is impossible because of the nonrational component in the experience which called forth the categorization in the first place.

To return, the main point is that the concept was learned, as language was developed, in relation to the variations of experience. A commonly held fallacy in philosophy is that though raw experience is chaotic and unclear, if one analyzes it, "unpacks" it, one will find it composed of a reasonable number of clear and distinct notions which made the experience possible. Thus, the fallacy goes on, one will arrive at some *a priori* faculty of knowledge which consists of these clear notions which are independent of all experience. This process is exemplified by the process which Kant suggested of mentally removing the accidental attributes of a body one by one—a process which, as mentioned earlier, simply cannot be carried out. If such clear notions are needed for such refined experience as human experience, this adds weight to the idea that clear notions are prior to all experience whatsoever. In fact, however, clarity is always the result of prodigious work with experience, using language as the tool of the task. The importance of stressing the role of language is that its importance is "repudiated" by Alfred North

Whitehead (1969) and entirely negated by philosopher of science Karl R. Popper:

> The conceptual system...provides merely a language for the theory...It cannot be made precise...Thus we are ultimately interested in theories and in their truth rather than in concepts and their meaning...If *concepts* are comparatively unimportant, *definitions* must also be unimportant. Thus although I am pleading here for *realism* in physics, I do not intend to define 'realism' or 'reality'. (Popper, 1967, p. 1314)

The present intent is to argue that the conceptual system itself, in the sense meant by Popper, is that which performs the *a priori* function of making apperception possible. Concepts are developed *a posteriori* from experience, but once established they serve as *a priori* organizers of new experience. Over the millennia, concepts and categories have developed as summations and systematizations of the ego's work with the *a posteriori*.

What, then, is truly given, and in what sense is it truly *a priori*? We may go back to the first building of a complex nucleus from primordial hydrogen (protons) for a clear example. To say that concepts are *a priori* would be like saying that a proton responds to being bombarded by another proton by means of a concept of combination, or by means of the concept of the "deuteron" that the two become in the process. The two respond in the interaction, not according to a concept, but according to *a priori*[4] patterns of

---

4. This is the correct use of *a priori* and it must be remembered that it is not rational, though it also holds the potentiality of rationality. Our description of it is rational.

potentiality which, at that level, are relatively limited in their possibilities for actualization.

As complexity builds, the patterns reveal greater potentials, but the potentiality for consciousness lacks the actual complexity at the earlier stage. Creative conceptualization is an attempt to understand effective-action-in-response-to-a-stimulus, and is thus always *a posteriori* because the concrete material, the stimulus *and* the response, is given first. Again, understanding is *getting used to*. This implies recurrence of the pattern which, in turn, implies a patterning element which is preconceptual. The patterning is also nonperceptual, for it is independent of perception in itself (recall the protons). Also, it can have a bewildering variety of representations within which a recognizable regularity is perceived, but none of which can be said fully to express the archetype (the pattern of *all* the potentials). It produces effects, and these are perceived and conceptualized.

It would be highly instructive in this regard to review the whole of evolution, from the primordial production of amino acids and nucleotides in proto-interplanetary space through all of the revolutions engendered by their interaction in the course of evolution. The revolutionary developments within this evolution, such as mobility, sexual reproduction, the conversion of the atmosphere to oxygen, cell specialization and predation, were all products of increased focusing of the protopsychoid potentialities of the evolving system of life, and each thus greatly speeded up the evolutionary process, essentially by utilizing more of the environmentally given energy sources for its own ends. What was thus achieved was a certain excess of energy, the very same *sort* of excess of energy which, at our level, we call "will power." When we have "excess energy" and are not merely surviving, that energy can be directed by choice rather than by pure necessity. Jung (1969c, pp. 182, 183) associated disposable libido with will power. Superior adaptability of the same sort as that which we now, at our level, have called conceptualization was also achieved, since at all levels this adaptability amounted to tools for organizing behavior, whether it was visual recognition of an enemy or of a herd or a family member.

Again, it was image earlier, language later, and concept later still. Concepts are abstractions from concrete experiences, and the word *abstraction* is an accurate one, pointing to the *a posteriori* nature of these concepts, though they now perform an *a priori* function for a developed individual. To give priority to axiomatic principles is like accepting the statement, "Well, after all, a star *solves the equations* of stellar interiors." That, a star does *not* do in the sense intended; what the star *does* do is to point to the *a priori* nature of an archetype whose function the equations attempt to envision. The analogy suffers from its own simplicity, but by substituting images of a more complex nature for the relatively simple mathematical equations,[5] we can begin to picture human behavior.

> What above all stultifies understanding is the arrant assumption that 'archetype' means an inborn idea. No biologist would ever dream of assuming that each individual acquires his general mode of behavior afresh each time. It is much more probable that the young weaver-bird builds his characteristic nest because he is a weaver bird and not a

5. For a star, this involves a simultaneous system of four second-order differential equations, solvable only by trial and error methods rather then by analytic ones, a fact which aids the analogy.

> rabbit. Similarly, it is more probable that man is born with a specifically human mode of behavior and not with that of a hippopotamus or with none at all. Integral to his characteristic behavior is his psychic phenomenology...Archetypes are typical forms of behavior which, once they become conscious, naturally present themselves as *ideas* and *images*, like everything else that becomes a content of consciousness. (Jung, 1969c, pp. 226f)

Since the archetypes, though few in number, are so varied in their imagery (as is also the case with concepts to a much lesser degree), they defy any exhaustive representation or conceptualization. They are, indeed, numinous as only that which is "other" can be. This, then, is what is given, or *a priori*, for humans: human archetypes which have been built upon the whole structure of evolutionary experience of life.

If experience is only complete by means of verbal concepts, we may appear to have come around a circular argument. But what is meant is that each human being achieves the conceptual basis of his or her relation to the world in the same way that humankind did as a whole: through image, language, and concept—though, as indicated above, the archetypal structure transcends these.

SPIRIT, MATTER, AND EGO-CONSCIOUSNESS

It has just been stated that the revolutions which speeded up the evolutionary process were "products of increased focusing of the protopsychoid potentialities of the evolving systems of life." This relation of centration (focusing) and complexification (development) has been documented at length by Pierre Teilhard de Chardin. The point is that pure causality cannot explain evolution, but that something which finds a *minimum* formulation in "protopsychoid potentialities" (which includes spirit) participates in the process, making evolutionary connections acausally.

> It is radically impossible to conceive that 'interiorized' and spontaneous elements could ever have developed from a universe presumed in its initial state to have consisted entirely of determinisms. Any who accepts this starting point blocks all roads that would bring him back to the present state of the universe. On the other hand, from a cosmos initially formed and made up of elementary 'freedoms,' it is easy to deduce...all the appearances of exactitude upon which the mathematical physics of matter if founded...The cosmos is fundamentally and primarily living. (Teilhard, 1969, p. 23)

The "present state," as it interests us, is characterized by ego-consciousness, that reflection which represents images to a finite mind. There can be no doubt that a mind which is sufficiently energetic to devote will and thought to abstractions is a new and unique sort of phenomenon in the cosmos. It is a situation which follows from the multicenteredness of the cosmos, combined with complexification. The God-circle "whose center is everywhere" describes not only the omnipresence of the divine or numinous element, but also the tendency of the cosmos to develop individuals.

The first symbol of the division of the cosmos into individual centers is the production of stars, for each is such a center of energy for the planetary life associated with it. But life itself also divides into centers. So far the most significant such development is the "human phenomenon," the individual

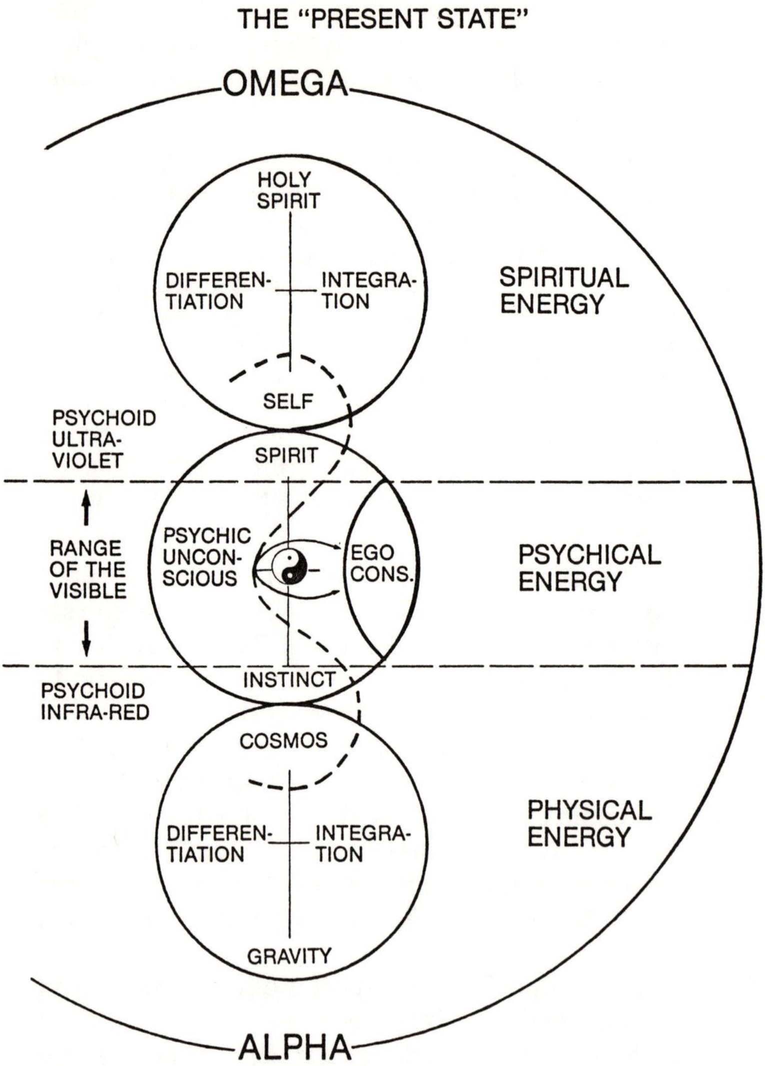

Figure 2. Spirit and Matter in Terms of the Development
of Ego-Consciousness.

self-reflexive consciousness. This development is stimulated by what is outside the developing organism throughout evolution, reaching its present stage in the development of concepts *a posteriori*, as noted above.

Indeed, this fact is the most telling evidence *for* the *a posteriori* development of concepts. By means of this reflection and its possible intercomparison with what is not-I, the ego is gradually differentiated from the rest of the cosmos. Then the ego can image the whole scope of the development of the cosmos, as well as its own emergence within that development. Figure 2 is a diagram both of the "present state" and of the process leading up to it in the universe.

In the diagram are presented three "quaternities," those of the energies of matter, psyche, and spirit. Encompassing the three is the circle of totality, or "cosmogenesis." Teilhard characterized cosmogenesis as the total interdevelopment of "tangential" (differentiating, dispersing) energy, and "radial" (complexifying, centrating, integrating) energy, *within which* are physical and spiritual energy. The tangential and radial dimensions are often called "horizontal" and "vertical" in theological usage, or perhaps we can, for our own times, say that tangential energy is that directed to economic development, while radial energy directs itself toward the actualization of *meaning*. Both of these dimensions, whatever terms we use for them, have both physical and spiritual aspects. The diagram shows this by placing both differentiating and integrating tendencies in both the physical energy and spiritual energy quaternities.

In one sense, the ego is a tangential development. This is the sense in which it can become differentiated from the cosmos. It is also the sense in which the *rest* of the cosmos becomes "meaning-space," but complementarily, the ego then becomes a focus of the purposefulness of the "protopsychoid potentialities" at work in the cosmos. The major question at hand is what the differentiation, which can also become a split-off-ness, amounts to. If there is anything to the diagram, it is not merely the *physical* world from which the ego is differentiated and can become cut off. That this is the case was brought out early in the chapter when it was pointed out that without the energy from the realm of *meaning* there would be no mediation of the physical world to consciousness at all.

With respect to the physical world, though, the split-off-ness manifests a different aspect from that which it shows with respect to the realm of meaning, or the focusing of life-potentials. Split-off-ness in the physical world leads to theoreticalism and ultrarationalism; in the realm of meaning it results in loss of psychic life or of meaning itself. All of this, however, anticipates the development to follow.

Regarding the spiritual-energy quaternity, we may say that the "self" exhibits complementary diversifying and focusing thrusts, both of which are taken as activities of spiritual energy and which relate the self to a unifying factor within and beyond it, which we might identify as that which we call "holy spirit." In Jungian terms this quaternity might be called "the incarnation of the *unity* of the holy spirit in the self," but "spiritual energy" is much more convenient.[6] At any rate, this quaternity is parallel to the physical energy quaternity within which physical *centration*

---

6. I am indebted to Aniela Jaffe for her presentation of the parallelisms of psychological and religious language in *The Myth of Meaning* (1970), Chapter 9.

and *complexification* are so easily seen. There, the above Jungian expression may also be translated quite rigorously into "the incarnation of the unity of gravity in the cosmos." Basically, the cosmos (matter and energy) is formed of positive forms of physical energy (matter and light), and negative energy represents the relatedness or boundness of the whole.[7]

The dynamic quality of both the spirit and matter quaternities is represented by the fact that both differentiation and integration are there as opposites. A physical example of this is the case of the photon which, if sufficiently energetic, can become two particles, one of matter and one of antimatter. These have opposite electric charges and so attract each other. They have been differentiated out of a single entity and seek to come together again.

The spiritual energy quaternity now provides unity to images and form to concepts, but prior to this, evolutionarily speaking, it provided patterning in cosmic, terrestrial, and biological development. The spiritual energy quaternity is really the spirit-aspect of the archetypes, as the physical energy quaternity is the matter-aspect. The evident applicability of physical laws to physical reality can be used as an argument that archetypes are the link between spirit and matter. This negates the Kantian assumption of an absolute split between the two. The archetypes which link the aspects of spirit and matter in the diagram would then be represented by circles con-

---

7. It is often assumed that the zero-point for gravitational potential energy is arbitrary, but the only common or universal point from which to measure it is the case of "infinite" separation of bodies. In that sense, gravitational energy is always negative. This has many interesting consequences, as pointed out by Marcel Golay in "Confessions of a Communications Engineer" (1961).

centric with the "conscious cosmogenesis" quaternity, but smaller. These circles would also be concentric with the psychic energy quaternity, surrounding it. One circle would relate "cosmos" and "self," another would relate physical and spiritual energies, and a third would relate "gravity" and "holy spirit." (See Figure 3.)

Continuing the parallelism of the two quaternities, self and cosmos are related through the symbol of the "circle whose center is everywhere [or infinitely plural] and whose circumference is nowhere," which has been mentioned at several points. This puts the holy spirit as the spiritual counterpart of gravity, responsible for psychic or spiritual centration (or unity), as gravity is in the physical sense.[8] Other parallels of holy spirit and gravity are documented by Jung.

That the development of the psyche depends upon gravity and the holy spirit was amplified in the early part of this chapter. If, therefore, an ego is split-off (egocentric), it loses much with respect to both of the "worlds." If, however, the ego can be "present" to

---

8. As the ultimate physical symbol of connection or inclusiveness, gravity can be further elaborated. It is the only fully cumulative force in the cosmos. Though it is the weakest of the four physical forces (gravitational, electromagnetic, weak nuclear, and strong nuclear), gravity is the dominant force in the cosmos because it is neither shielded nor saturable—all stellar evolution is a response to it. It is, again, a symbol of unity, of the whole, or of the one. On the other hand, the stars (and galaxies) are the ultimate physical symbol of the many, or of differentiation or the pull-apart (in many directions). They are evidence of the ubiquitousness of the center of the cosmos. Stars speak to us of distance, separation and aloneness, but within a whole, or rather in levels of relationship: pairs, clusters, galaxies, and the cosmos. Thus we have also a symbol of the fact that the overall inclusion includes the separation, for gravity also causes the separation of the stars.

THE "PRESENT STATE"

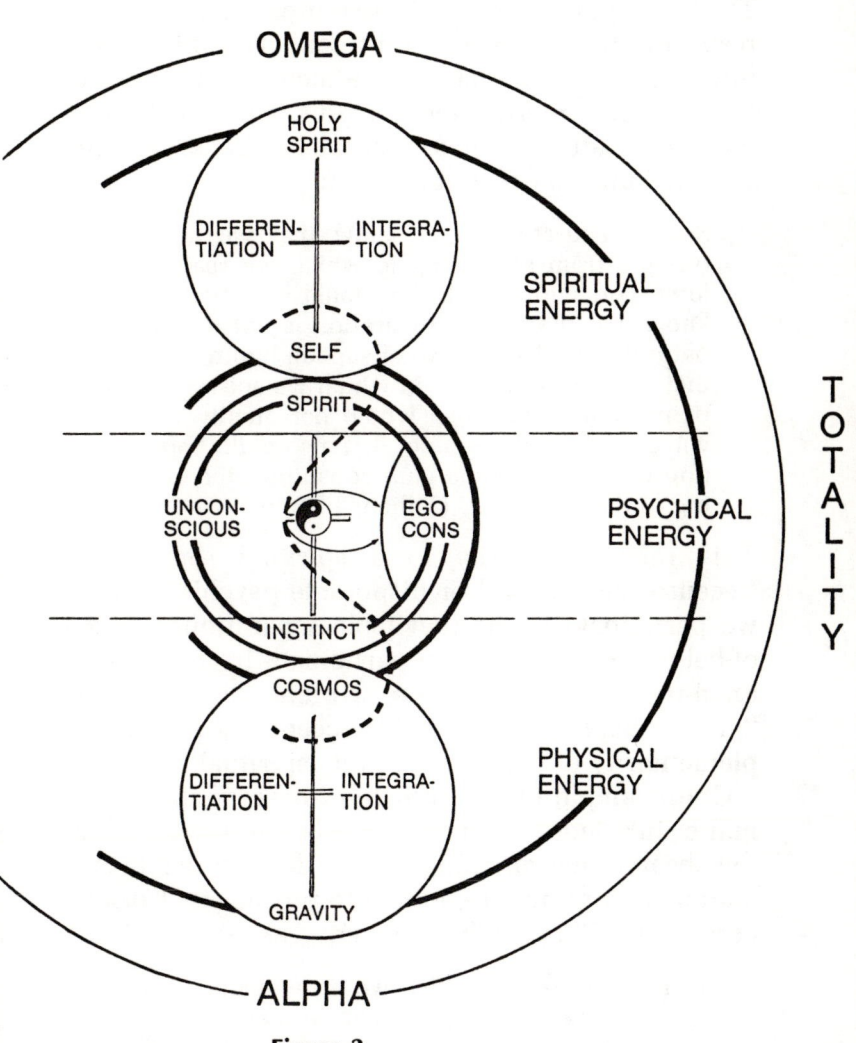

Figure 3

its inner world, which mediates both "matter" and "holy spirit" to it via "instinct" and "spirit" on the diagram, it can gain its own life in a greater context. The two separations and the two presences, i.e., with respect to the two worlds represented by the quaternities of matter and spirit, are mentioned together, for they are interdependent. Still, we can discuss their individual effects separately. Take, for instance, Tillich's definition of sin:

> *Sin is separation*...We know that we are estranged from something to which we really belong, and with which we *should* be united. We know that the fate of separation is not merely a natural event like a flash of sudden lightning, but that it is an experience in which we actively participate, in which our whole personality is involved, and that, as such, it is also *guilt*. Separation which is fate *and* guilt constitutes the meaning of the word 'sin.' (Tillich, 1948, p. 153)

This refers primarily to a spiritual separation. Because there is will or disposable psychic energy, we participate in the inevitable separation-in-spite-of-belonging, and we *can* participate in the acceptance-in-spite-of-separation which Tillich calls "grace." Separation and being accepted are the complementarity of ego-cosmos in its spiritual form.

One example of the split-apart-ness of spirit and matter in science might be helpful here. The fact that the observer has anything at all to do with reality is a matter of continuing concern to physicists. Heisenberg quotes Einstein (from memory) as saying to him:

> You are speaking of what we know about nature and no longer about what nature really does. In science we ought to be concerned solely with what nature does. (Heisenberg, 1971, p. 68)

Here the split is obvious: science cannot be concerned with what nature "really does" without knowing about nature, yet that is what Einstein, as quoted, wants us to attempt.

The flow of images and energy to the ego always consists of elements of both matter and spirit coming together in a meaningful way. The matter is present even if only in the aeons of evolutionary experience which formed our intellectual and emotional faculties. If science studies matter and religion studies spirit, we thus have a unified picture in which the ego's relation to religion is completely parallel to its relation to science, and we have a picture of the complementarities in each. Thus, also, we have seen what the ego-complex is split off from, when it is split-off or egocentric, and what it is present-to when it is functioning as differentiated but present. This amounts to a justification of the complementary treatment of science and religion as ways of knowing reality.

4
Complementarity

With rack and screw I put Nature through
   A thorough inquisition:
But She was so afraid that if I were disappointed
I should hurt Her more that Her answers were
disjointed—
   I did. I didn't. I will. I won't.
She is just as big a liar, in fact, as we are.
   To discover how to be truthful now
   Is the reason I follow this star.
                    W. H. Auden, "For the Time Being"

This chapter has no settling place in the main development of this book and has long wandered among the other chapters. At the same time it is a cornerstone for the whole, for it provides the model by means of which the rest can be understood. Indeed, without the reality of complementarity the rest would appear quite irrational. But the nonrationality of reality is fact—hard physical fact—so that the wandering cornerstone must find a place to stay.

The problem is that the nonrational seems always to be worming its way into our attempts to reduce the world to order and rationality. Specifically, the nonrational somehow finds its way into philosophy and mathematics as well as into theology and physics. It now seems possible to say why this occurs, for the problem has taken a singularly acute form in physics.

That there are opposites (conscious/unconscious, spirit/matter, good/evil, and the others) is not the problem, but rather that *single* things must be described in terms of such opposites. Without these contradictory descriptive terms, the description is incomplete. As modern a philosopher as Whitehead rejected the notion that a situation can require contradictory concepts in its description. He repudiated the belief that "logical inconsistencies can indicate anything else than some antecedent errors." (Whitehead, 1969, pp. vii, viii)

Whitehead's point of view here is characteristic of 19th century thought. In the 20th century, first in physics and then in mathematics, this kind of thinking has begun to give way under the pressure of evidence and theoretical proof. Since the primary aim of this chapter is to describe the evidence found in quantum physics, the work in mathematics will be mentioned briefly here at the beginning.

Two years after Whitehead wrote the words quoted above, Gödel proved that finite logical systems of a certain minimum complexity cannot be shown to be free of contradiction. A finite system is one which has a limited number of axioms for its foundation. Gödel also proved that there will always be true statements which should be included in the system but which remain outside unless they are incorporated as new axioms. At one stroke, then, he proved that in order to be complete, a system must be infinitely complex, i.e., have an infinite number of axioms, and that such a system could not be shown to be internally consistent.

It had also long been proven that if a statement and its formal contradiction are both derivable by (correct) deduction from a given set of axioms, then any statement is correctly derivable. Therefore it would seem that Gödel has given a deathblow to all logical limitation of thought. This is precisely what Whitehead was aiming at in his repudiation above.

But now that it is known that internal consistency cannot be guaranteed and that logical systems are always essentially incomplete, what is to be done? The point of view taken here is that one must begin in the middle and base theoretical work upon facts rather than upon arbitrary axioms. That is also why the major weight of this chapter is given to physics.

Yet it is to be noted that even the facts of physics are secondary in importance to the guiding fact of this book—that consciousness has arisen out of that which is unconscious. The physics provides a model for thought—that of complementarity—for viewing all situations in which contradictions arise in the description of single entities. At the close of the chapter, that model will be applied directly to the relationship of consciousness to that which is unconscious.

COMPLEMENTARITY IN PHYSICS

The problem is that a single entity exhibits contradictory characteristics. The knowledge that this is the case has arisen in the attempts of physicists to interpret the results of the two experiments (and variations upon them) described in Appendix A. The experiments were designed to answer the question as to what concepts apply to the basic recognized constituents of the physical world, energy and matter. Ordinary visible light was taken as representative of energy, and the electron was seen as the easiest-to-handle representative of matter. It was thought that energy would be a "wave" phenomenon, i.e., would exhibit *continuity*, and that matter was "atomic," i.e., particulate or *discontinuous*. By means of the experiments, however, it was discovered that both entities, light and electrons, exhibited both of the contradictory aspects, continuity, and discontinuity, though they did not exhibit both simultaneously.

Actually, one kind of experiment *excluded discontinuity* for light when done with light, and for electrons when done with electrons. The other kind *excluded continuity* for light and electrons. In these two terms, *continuity* and *discontinuity*, the logical contradiction or mutual exclusiveness of those two theories is made clear.

Thus we have two experiments, both of which, after over sixty years of refinement and discussion, are considered correct and factual. Each absolutely excludes the theory which is the necessary basis for the explanation of the other—necessary, that is, if we *must* think in such terms as waves and particles. On this point, Nobel laureate Richard Feynman emphasizes, "*All* our experience is with waves and particles." The wave and particle natures are *two sides of one thing* whose nature cannot be rationally expressed. This one thing is *light*, which seems both continuous and discontinuous, and which the experiments show is neither continuous nor discontinuous, but which we *know* at a level beyond rational knowledge is a unity.

Physicist Max Jammer, who will shortly be quoted more fully, says of this situation that we are "applying to the description of a physical phenomenon two categories of notions which, strictly speaking, are contradictory to each other." We must distinguish between this logical ("hard") contradiction and mutual exclusion ("soft" contradiction). The former strictly applies to descriptive concepts in conflict *at an instant of time*. Mutual exclusion is less strong in that it says that the contradictory aspects cannot arise simultaneously but can arise successively. Which of the two aspects is exhibited depends upon the experiment, and the experiments which give the contradictory results *cannot* be set up simultaneously. Since the contradictory concepts cannot be brought into rigorous conflict simultaneously, it might be thought that mutual exclusion is as strong a statement as can be made about the complementarity of the descriptive situation. This brings us to the heart of the problem.

It is contended here that we have a case of the stronger criterion of logical contradiction, for it is a single entity which exhibits the two aspects, wave and particle, continuity and discontinuity. A physicist who does either of the two kinds of experiments uses the *same* source of light (or the *same* source of electrons) in both. The experiments indicate both a wave nature *and* a particle nature for light. The light is thus *one thing* with two contradictory aspects. We may say, as physicists do, that light *travels* as a wave and *interacts* as a particle, but between traveling and interacting is a qualitative "leap" into a *contradictory* aspect. Thus we may truly say that there is a problem in the description of light. These last sentences could be repeated by replacing *light* with *electrons,* so that there is the same problem in the description of the latter.

The succinct presentation by Edward Teller of the notion of complementarity (Chapter Two) employs no technical terms whatsoever:

> The idea of complementarity is that in order to describe a situation you have to use (at least on certain occasions) two mutually exclusive approaches. If you omit either, the description is incomplete. Both must be used. Because they are

> mutually exclusive, it is necessary to adjust the two approaches in a manner that is by no means obvious. (Teller, 1969, p. 83)

Here is a more precise, but more extended amplification by Jammer:

> It was this mutual exclusion and, at the same time, indispensability of fundamental notions and descriptions which led Bohr to the conclusion that the problem with which quantum physics found itself confronted could not be solved by merely modifying or reinterpreting traditional conceptions. What was needed, he concluded, was a new logical instrument. He called it 'complementarity,' denoting thereby the logical relation between two descriptions or sets of concepts which, though mutually exclusive, are nevertheless both necessary for an exhaustive description of the situation. In Heisenberg's reciprocal uncertainty relations[1] he saw a mathematical expression which defines the extent to which complementary notions may overlap, that is, may be applied simultaneously, but, of course, not rigorously. The uncertainty relations, Bohr contended, tell us the price we have to pay for violating the rigorous exclusion of notions, the price for applying to the description of a physical phenomenon two categories of notions which, strictly speaking, are contradictory to each other. (Jammer, 1966, p. 348)

Because Teller's formula is so concise, we will use the phrase "Teller's formula" in the succeeding pages and chapters to recall all of the qualitative statements used in support of the points discussed in this section. Indeed, the formula contains words which can be used as "recall-triggers" for all of them.

From the two statements just quoted, we will begin

---

1. See Appendix B for a discussion of complementarity and the uncertainty principle.

to describe characteristics of complementarity, amplifying with other sources as we proceed.

In an earlier work (Hitchcock, 1976) I developed nine characteristics of complementarity of which the following apply to the present discussion.

(a) Completeness of description requires both contradictory aspects to be incorporated. They are neither synthesized nor superseded. They are (1) *mutually exclusive* but (2) *both necessary*. Since a complete description requires both contradictory aspects to be incorporated, the words *incomplete* or *approximate* separability of the contradictory concepts applying to a microphysical entity will also be used to indicate the property (a-2). And, if "perfection" can be identified with the absence of contradiction, we might say that *completeness requires imperfection*.

(b) The *observer is essentially involved* in the situation which he or she is attempting to observe or to know.

(c) The unity behind the complementary conceptual opposites is not ultimately susceptible of a rationalistic description (at least as complementarity stands). It is a *nonrational unity*.

(d) The single entity exhibits both aspects so that *reversal* (or exchange) of aspect occurs—a qualitative "leap" into the contradictory manifestation.

(e) As a universal principle, *causality is denied*, at least within complementarity as developed here. This will be seen as following from the ultimate inseparability of the object or entity from the instrument through which knowledge of the nature of the entity is obtained.

(f) There is an essential dynamism or disequilibrium in the complementarity of contradictory aspects of entities, though this is not explicit in the statement to be quoted. This characteristic is not considered essential to the argument of this study, but helpful insights can be obtained by carrying it along.

(a) Let us consider the first point. Jammer's words, "concepts which, though mutually exclusive, are nevertheless both necessary[2] for an exhaustive description," and Teller's "both must be used" (for completeness), as related to the nature of a *single* entity (the photon of light, or the electron), point to the *relatedness of opposites* in spite of the exclusion.

(a-1) In emphasizing that both opposites are necessary, Holton stresses their "irreducibility" or the impossibility of "attempting to dissolve one member of the pair in the other" as essential to Bohr's point of view: specifically, Bohr asked that physicists accept both [antithetical descrip-

---

2. Gerhard Adler, in "Basic Concepts of Analytical Psychology" quotes a letter of Jung's with similar import:

> The language I speak must be ambiguous, must have two meanings in order to be fair to the dual aspect of our psychic nature. I strive quite consciously and deliberately for ambiguity of expression, because it is superior to unequivocality and reflects the nature of life. My whole temperament inclines me to be very unequivocal indeed. That is not difficult, but it would be at the cost of truth. I purposely allow all the overtones and undertones to be heard, partly because they are there anyway, and partly because they give a fuller picture of reality. Unequivocality makes sense only in establishing facts, but not in interpreting them.

Adler goes on to say:

> One is reminded of a remark by the physicist Niels Bohr that there is a relationship of *complementarity* between the clarity and the rightness of a statement, so much so that a statement which is too clear always contains something false. (Adler, 1974, p. 15)

tions]—though both would not be found in the same
plane of focus at any given time[3] (1973, p. 133).

Holton stresses Bohr's view that the contradictory
but necessary themes are not to be converted, or
mutually absorbed, into a single new entity but remain as an *either/or* (recalling Kierkegaard). This
either/or appears as nature putting a situation of
choice before physicists as to which information will
be tested for and which will be excluded. Physicists
did not like this at all. They wanted to have all information which might be applied to, or obtained from,
a phenomenon *at once*. Teller's words "both must be
used" and Jammer's "overlap" increase the sense of
"both/and." Our knowledge that it is *light*, a unity, or
electron, another unity, to which the opposites apply,
emphasize a "both/and" which links the two and
highlights their contradictory character.

Two statements may be made here regarding the
relation of soft and hard contradiction, which indicate that the latter possibly is the case. First, there
is the degree of "both/and" mentioned just above

---

3. Holton has discussed this in terms of what he calls "themata,"
a dimension different from both of the usually accepted components of scientific work, observation and theory, but equally
necessary to that work.

> This third dimension is the dimension of fundamental
> presuppositions, notions, terms, methodological judg-
> ments and decisions—in short, of themata or themes—
> which are themselves neither directly evolved from, nor
> resolvable into, objective observation on the one hand,
> or logical, mathematical, and other formal ratiocination
> on the other hand (Holton, 1973, p. 57).

He calls these themata, or the thematic dimension:

> an active and necessary component that is effective in
> scientific work, both on the personal and on the insti-
> tutional level—preconceptions that appear to be un-
> avoidable for scientific thought, but are not themselves
> verifiable or falsifiable (1973, p. 23).

which brings the opposites to a clash. This means that we have exhibited at least a certain *level* of logical contradiction, for, as Jammer says, the concepts within the repertoire of light and electrons are contradictory.

Secondly, we can exhibit mathematical expressions such as:

$$E = A/\lambda \quad \text{or} \quad p = B/\lambda,$$

Both of these equations are known to apply to photons and electrons. It is well known that the left side of each equation expresses a measurable quantity which logically belongs to the *particle nature* of light, being a definite, discrete amount of energy (E) or momentum (p) in accordance with the precision to which the wavelength (λ) is known. A and B are constants with suitable units. But λ is logically a *wave* property. There is no doubt that these equations are intended to apply *at an instant*. As was mentioned earlier, the more precisely the wavelength expresses a pure wave nature (by its having a single pure value), the more precisely the energy or momentum expresses a pure particle nature (by being definite and discrete). Thus, these equations embody a logical contradiction via a juxtaposition of the opposites. While pure logic may well support its claim to be free of empirical content, the various philosophies taken as a whole can no more do so than can physics, for they work with verbal language and concepts of human concern.

(a-2) Given that our concepts of microphysical entities are approximately applicable to reality, but *only* approximately, it follows that the complementary concepts, while logically opposed, are only approximately separable *as applied* to phenomena. That is, the logical opposition can be decisively established, but *there are no objects corresponding to only one of the opposites absolutely exclusively.* This point is seen as related to the phrase in the verbal formulation of complementarity wherein it is stated that a complete or exhaustive description requires both concepts.

The approximate separability of the concepts is witnessed by Jammer's word *overlap* with respect to the complementary notions which, in logical terms, "strictly speaking, are contradictory."

Again, the formulae, $E = A/\lambda$ and $p = B/\lambda$ *link* the particle and wave concepts together in single expressions, so that one cannot describe a microphysical particle without the wave concept entering the description, and vice versa.

A "rationalistic" view might be defined as one for which this mixture of contradictory concepts is an "imperfection." That many scholars take a rationalistic attitude is clearly evident in the empirical fact that a great deal of energy is expended toward ridding microphysics of the sort of contradiction at issue here, as distinct from ridding it of errors. In Bohr's words, the linking of conceptual opposites *is* an "irrationality," the very opposite of rationalistic perfection, though he urges us to accept the situation, not as ineradicable error, but for the sake of completeness and as the way things are. Hence the keyword: completeness requires imperfection.

(b) The essential involvement of the observer in the situation where we desire physical knowledge has been stated by Jammer as

> Von Neumann's far-reaching conclusion that it is not possible to formulate the laws of quantum mechanics in a complete and consistent way without a reference to human consciousness. Von Neumann fully realized that this conceptual pro-

cedure led to the inexorable result that "experience only makes statements of this type: an observer has made a certain (subjective) observation; and never any like this: a physical quantity has a certain value," or, as Heisenberg once said, the laws of nature which we formulate mathematically in quantum theory deal no longer with the particles themselves but with our knowledge of the elementary particles. (Jammer, 1966, p. 373)

By contrast, Einstein's position was: "Physics is an attempt conceptually to grasp reality as it is thought independently of its being observed" (Einstein, 1949, p. 81). But Bohr (1934) emphasizes that as we probe into the microphysical realm, our usual capacity for distinguishing between objects and our *observation* of the objects can no longer be maintained:

The impossibility of distinguishing in our customary way between physical phenomena and their observation places us, indeed, in a position quite similar to that which is so familiar in psychology where we are continually reminded of the *difficulty of distinguishing between subject and object.* (Bohr, 1934, p. 15)

Here, we take the statement of the impossibility of a final extrication of the observer from the observed as indicating the essential involvement of the observer, which is the point at hand.

Though not explicit in Teller's formulation, this involvement is implied in his phrase "by no means obvious" in relation to a possible "adjustment" of the two complementary "approaches."[4] It is the ob-

4. If mutually exclusive conceptualizations of light or electrons could be adjusted so as to be *uniquely* applicable at specifiable times, or in specifiable experimental situations, we would have achieved a *final* adjustment of the complementary pairs. But we have indicated that both the uncertainty principle, and the for-

server's *choice* as to which of the complementary aspects will be exhibited, by means of his or her chosen experimental approach to the physical situation to be described. We will take this to be what is meant by the phrase "by no means obvious," for where the choice is obvious, there really isn't choice.

(c) The reasons for considering that the contradictory conceptualizations apply to a unity, i.e., an entity such as "electron" or "light," were given above. Therefore, either of these entities is nonrational in itself. This is indicated simply by the fact that in interpreting our observations we seem to find it necessary to apply both of the contradictory concepts to it. That is, we ask the question, "What is the nature of light?" and the account of what we know about it contains irreconcilable opposites. As Teller says, "Both must be used," and Jammer uses the expression "equally necessary" which he takes from Bohr, as will be seen just below.

Though these authors do not speak *explicitly* of the unity behind the opposites, we will consider this unity as nonetheless implied by the statements which they make in describing the problem of conceptualizing light or electrons, for each of these statements carries such an implication when contradictory aspects are applied to it. The unity discussed here is the same as the level of reality called "archetypal" in Chapter Two.

Bohr does, however, use the word *irrational* with respect to a unity, when he says:

---

mulae $E = 2 \times 10^{-16}/\lambda$ and $p = 6.63 \times 10^{-27}/\lambda$ bring the hopefully excluded concept into every situation to which complementarity applies, so that, as complementarity is presently understood, a final adjustment of these conceptualizations in such cases is impossible.

> It is maintained that the fundamental postulate of the indivisibility of the quantum of action is itself, from the classical point of view, an irrational element which inevitably requires us to forego a causal mode of description and which, because of the coupling between phenomena and their observation, forces us to adopt a new mode of description designated as *complementary* in the sense that any given application of classical concepts precludes the simultaneous use of other classical concepts which in a different connection are equally necessary for the elucidation of the phenomena. (Bohr, 1934, p. 10)

(d) Given that a microphysical entity can manifest each of its complementary aspects at different times, we are not surprised to observe from time to time that the aspect which is apparently dominant at a given moment will give way to its opposite. Physicists say, for example, that a photon *travels* according to its wave aspect, but *interacts* according to its particle aspect. This reversal of aspect is also evident in the realm of psychology, as often pointed out by Jung and Erich Neumann.

Perhaps there is a single, general archetypal process of manifestation by means of particles, and the many examples which we know of this process of manifestation are simply many faces of one very general process.

(f) Characteristic (a-2) involves the impossibility of a complete separability of complementary concepts. On the other hand, as quoted in a note to the discussion of the characteristic (a-1), Holton stresses that the particles are "irreducible" to each other, cannot be "mutually absorbed" into each other. Taken with Teller's comment that the adjustment of their relation to each other is "by no means obvious," this suggests a *dynamic interplay* of the complementary concepts as properties of the single entity which manifests them. The sixth characteristic, the phenomenon of reversal of aspect, aids this suggestion of a situation wherein no final equilibrium is to be found.

THE COMPLEMENTARITY OF EGO AND UNCONSCIOUS

As they relate to physics, psychology, and philosophy, the relations between ego-consciousness and that which is unconscious are usually seen as between the ego and physical reality, or between the ego and spiritual reality, as an attempt on the ego's part to discover what is "out there" or "in there," respectively. In these sciences the ego inevitably disturbs that which it is attempting to observe. In the case of psychology, von Franz states it as follows:

> Bohr's idea of complementarity is especially interesting to Jungian psychologists, for Jung saw that the relationship between the conscious and unconscious mind also forms a complementary pair of opposites. Each new content that comes up from the unconscious is altered in its basic nature of being partly integrated into the conscious mind of the observer...And each enlargement of the observer's consciousness caused by (say) dream interpretation has again an immeasurable repercussion and influence on the unconscious. Thus the unconscious can only be approximately described (like the particles of microphysics) by paradoxical concepts. What it really is "in itself" we shall never know, just as we shall never know this about matter. (Jung, 1964b, p. 308)

Although spiritual reality and physical reality have a complementary relationship to *each other*, it should be borne in mind that we are here discussing the relation of the ego to the unconscious, which includes both of these realities, though the discussion, for the most part, must deal with one at a time when seeking concrete examples.

For the following comparison, the portions are numbered according to the characteristics of complementarity given earlier in Chapter Four.

(a-1) That the ego, as defined by the criterion of consciousness, is opposed to the unconscious is evident from the terms *conscious* and *unconscious* themselves. In addition to the hard contradiction in the terms, there is a sort of dynamic mutual exclusion which prefers that these two not meet, that they go their own ways in daily life. This is due to still another kind of imperfection, that of suffering in the meeting. Von Franz discusses this clearly:

> When the Self and the ego come together and get in touch with each other, who is wounded? As soon as they come together both are wounded because to get in touch with the ego is a partial damage to the symbol of the Self, just as it is a partial damage of the ego to get in touch with the Self. These two entities cannot meet without damaging each other. For the Self, you could say that one way in which it is damaged is that instead of being a potential wholeness it becomes a partial reality; in part it becomes real within the individuated person—in the realising actions and words of the person. That is a restriction for the Self and its possibilities. The ego, however, is wounded because something greater breaks into its life. We generally think of that part, which is why Dr. Jung says that it means tremendous suffering to get in touch with the process of individuation. It causes a tremendous wound because, put simply, we are robbed of the capacity for arranging our own lives according to our own wishes. (Von Franz, 1966, v. 17)

Suffering is thus seen as part of the religious function of the ego, but warning must be given that this suffering has nothing to do with *resignation* to suffering, which does not have an active conscious quality. Nor is suffering sought as a means to individuation or fulfillment. This would mistake a mere concomitant to the process either with a means or with an end.

(a-2) In Chapter Six we will describe the process of the emergence of ego-consciousness out of the unconscious, which is equivalent to establishing that it does so. It should be clear that there is not a complete break, but to emphasize the point, we return to a statement quoted in Chapter Three:

> ...there is a consciousness in which unconsciousness predominates, as well as a consciousness in which self-consciousness predominates...There is no conscious content which can be with absolute certainty said to be totally conscious, for that would necessitate an unimaginable totality of consciousness (Jung, 1969c, p. 188).

Consideration of the diagrams in Chapters Two and Three showing the dependency of the ego on the unconscious also supports this comparison. The quotation from von Franz above states the same interdependence.

(b) Since the observer *is* the conscious part—the ego—this point is established. There is no outside or extrapsychic point from which to observe the conscious part as such. That which is unconscious cannot know that it is unconscious. This also applies to the great differences among humans regarding their consciousness. The emergence of consciousness and the assimilation of the unconscious is a continuing process of a highly individual character (which is why Jung calls it "individuation"). This, in itself, exemplifies the absence of a "final adjustment." But here the writings are so copious that one may refer to the entry "individuation" in the index of any of Jung's works.

(c) The unity behind the opposites was discussed in Chapter Two as "archetypal reality." Reasons were given there for saying that this unity is preconceptual and numinous. The archetype remains preconceptual, which is precisely nonrational.

(d) The process of reversal of aspect is well attested. The sudden change of an image or thought from conscious to unconscious or vice versa is sufficient evidence. Or, pathologically, the ego may be submerged in an archetype or identified with it. Various forms of inspiration and visions also are evidence. Especially important is the fact that though the psychic is defined by *will*, or excess energy, the unconscious also may be described as manifesting a will by means of the pressures which it exerts on ego-consciousness. The relation between these wills is one of the central problems of the individuating psyche. Here we would say that consciousness emerges in terms of opposites based on the fact that we have the duality of spiritual reality and physical reality in the unconscious. Jung has said in several places[5] that the tension of opposites is empirically the most favorable condition for the emergence of consciousness. As von Franz states, this emergence has tremendous *mutual* repercussions, although it is impossible to state what the unconscious as a whole is *becoming*, and this can be said of consciousness as well.

(e) The fact that complementarity denies causality as an ultimate principle in physics was not discussed

5. Notably in *Psychology and Religion* (1969b, pp. 459-461), and in *Memories, Dreams and Reflections* (1963, p 345).

above under complementarity in physics, for it is quite technical. Nevertheless, the lack of an ultimate causal priority in the relationship of ego and unconscious is important, as can be seen in Jung's words:

> The behavior of the archetypes cannot be investigated at all without the interaction of the observing consciousness. Therefore the question as to whether the process is initiated by consciousness or by the unconscious archetype can never be answered; unless, in contradiction to experience, one either robbed the archetype of its autonomy or degraded consciousness into a mere machine. We find ourselves in best agreement with psychological experience if we concede to the archetype a definite measure of independence, and to consciousness a degree of creative freedom proportionate to its scope. There then arises that reciprocal action between two relatively autonomous factors which compels us, when describing and explaining the processes, to present sometimes the one and sometimes the other factor as the acting subject, even when God becomes [hu]man. (Jung, 1969b, p. 479)

(f) The whole discussion in Chapter Six of the emergence of consciousness will display the essential dynamism of the process. As in physics, opposites are produced when the energy is sufficient and the conditions for manifestation are fulfilled. Looking back over the process as it has developed to date, one cannot find a single point of absolute equilibrium.

As an addendum to this demonstration of the complementarity of the conscious and the unconscious, the notion of "objectivity" can be clarified. That which is objective is, strictly speaking, that which is beyond the subject's will. The notion can only arise insofar as there is a subject with a sense of autonomy so that there can also be a sense of limitation of will. The border between the subjective and the objective is seldom well defined; hence some of the acts which seem to the subject to arise from will can be seen by others as collective behavior, i.e., approximately automatic, rather than individual behavior denoting a conscious will.

The realm of the objective, thus defined, can be divided into two regions: the outer-objective which we call the *a posteriori*, and the inner-objective which we call the *a priori*. Kant's "categories" conform to this notion of the inner-objective, their nature, according to him, being absolutely beyond the will of the subject. These days we are more likely to note dreams, instinctual behavior, and archetypal behavior as things at least initially beyond the will and certainly never wholly integrated to the realm of conscious will. In addition, there are at least the autonomous complexes documented by Jung and the intuitive solution to scientific problems documented by Poincaré, Agazziz, and others.

A Symbol for the Complementarity Relationship

The basic Chinese symbol for the connected oppositeness of things is the *t'ai chi t'u* or "diagram of the Great Ultimate."

The two colors stand for the two polar opposites, yin and yang, which take on the many qualities noted previously. The purpose of the enclosed dots of the other color is to show both the *essential* incompleteness of the differentiation of opposing concepts, and that, in fact, the opposite is to be found hidden at the heart of any differentiated concept. Knowledge and belief, for example, oppose each other, yet lie at each other's center, whether one speaks of observations, axioms, or revelation.

Axiomatic-deductive knowledge implies belief in the axioms as self-evident. Such belief is grounded in knowledge of a different sort—that derived from everyday experience (though one intends to depart a great way from everyday experience in one's deductions). Everyday experience is founded in a belief in an external world (though some philosophy challenges this) and so on and on. We can, of course, believe that we can claim the right to choose whatever axioms we please, but only at the cost of the ideal principle of the agreement of knowledge with its object; we *must* derive our axioms from observation if we desire to have knowledge which will agree with the physical world. And, of course, language is as objective as the physical world—i.e., it can no more be freely chosen than physical facts can.

To return to the symbol of the *t'ai chi t'u*. Its deficiency is that it is not convenient for representing the complementary relation of particular polar opposites. For that reason, I have adapted the symbol of the "Moving yang line" ⬅–⊖–➤ from the *I Ching* by adding arrows. For example:

Knowledge ⬅–⊖–➤ Belief

In the *I Ching*, a yang line is continuous (——) and the yin line is broken (— —) indicating their respective qualities of masculinity and femininity, as discussed earlier. The term *moving* or *old* or *stressed* as applied to a line means that there is an incipient change of the quality into its opposite, yang into yin or yin into yang, and is indicated by –⊖– (old yang), and —x— (old yin). Thus, the symbol ◄⊖► has both a static situational and a dynamic changing quality.

As an application in physics, we might express the complementarity of the wave and particle concepts as: wave ◄⊖► particle. Other important examples in physics are those quantities which are related by the uncertainty principle. Certain pairs of measurable quantities are linked together because the attempt to measure one of them destroys our knowledge of the other. One such pair is spatial location and momentum. If we attempt a very precise measurement of *where* a particle is, we give it a kick which destroys our knowledge of its speed and direction of motion. Another pair is the energy of a system and the time at which it has the measured energy. Again, measurement of either destroys knowledge of the other. For each pair singly, we would denote their complementarity thus:

$$\text{spatial location} \quad ◄⊖► \quad \text{momentum}$$

$$\text{energy} \quad ◄⊖► \quad \text{time}$$

Though these pairs are mutually exclusive as to knowledge, they remain related. In physics they are even called "conjugate pairs."

As will be discussed again in Chapter Five, the quantities in the two pairs are also cross-related. The relationship of space and time, for instance, is well known. Energy and momentum are related in very deep ways, but most simply in the fact that they are the quantities most fundamentally *conserved* in the cosmos. But the conservation laws turn out, in quantum theory, to be related to still another and deeper kind of regularity on the theoretical side: the symmetry of laws of physics.

The observed fact, for example, that the laws are symmetrical for translation (change of place) in

> space, when we add the principles of quantum mechanics, turns out to mean that *momentum is conserved*. That the laws are symmetrical under translation in time means, in quantum mechanics, that *energy* is conserved. (Feynman, 1963, p. 52-3)

This is a new dimension of the linking of the theoretical and observational via quantum mechanics. Theoretical symmetry and observed conservation mutually imply each other. Note in the quotation that, again, space is linked to momentum and energy to time, the same pairs of canonical conjugates related by the uncertainty principle. But since space and time are linked in our thought, and Einstein's relativity theory shows that they are radically inseparable, let us tie the two pairs together in the following diagram:

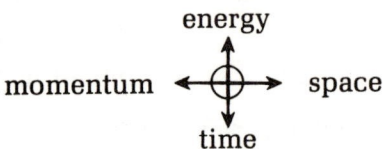

As a *whole*, the four carry great meaning and the diagram summarizes their intimate relationship. Moreover, as Jung noted in *Aion* (1959, p. 242), two lines crossing denote a center or a focus which points beyond the four peripheral symbols. Psychologically, one does not just arbitrarily divide a line into two by means of a point but seeks another objective line by means of which a mutual division into halves is achieved. The quaternities which result, such as this one, are very helpful in summarizing and relating ideas in a way similar to the way in which mathematical relations summarize and relate quantities, and the quaternities carry the symbolic function of mediating psychic energy as discussed in

Chapter Five. Jung has shown that quaternities play a significant role in this experience.

The Chinese *t'ai chi t'u* shows that the idea of complementarity is really very old. One might well ask what is added by physics and mathematics. What is added is *phenomenological grounding*. Whereas the complementary interaction of yin and yang is an intuitive truth, we now have very precise, hard physical fact. Until our attempt to rationalize the cosmos came to grief in modern sciences, it could be maintained that the cosmos was fundamentally rational. Now, however, the more carefully and thoroughly the reality is pursued in science, the more it becomes clear that the universe is not fundamentally rational, but rather a balance of rational and nonrational. While complementarity is very ancient, it is now on a new and solid foundation.[6]

---

6. Recent evidence has made complementarity very solid indeed. Physicist John S. Bell developed a mathematical relationship now known as "Bell's inequality," which predicts the experimental possibility of distinguishing between the quantum-mechanical interpretation employed in this book and its rivals. Bernard D'Espagnat (1979) reported the experimental results which uniformly favor the present interpretation.

5

Spirit-Matter

Without contraries is no progression.
William Blake, *The Marriage of Heaven and Hell*

The primary purpose of this chapter is to show spirit as both pattern and evolutionary entelechy within matter. Related to this purpose is a demonstration of the role of number in patterning, i.e., in the organization of matter. Since Jung has shown that the numbers 3 and 4 play such an important role in the psyche, it is of the greatest interest to see how these numbers arise also in physics. We will look at the numerical aspects of patterning first. This will lead naturally to the material on the evolution of spirit-matter in the cosmos.

Spirit is patterning, as we will see, but it is not just a plan. As patterning, spirit governs the universe, is dynamic and can move matter. It has the ability to organize matter into the patterns we observe: the shapes of galaxies, stars, planets, atoms, crystalline structures, etc. The energy relationships of things and the coherences of all sorts which we find in nature are determined by spirit. But we must go further than this to include the evolution and behavior of *all* living forms. Jung described human behavior in terms of archetypes, which are the irrepresentable nuclei of the major collective aspects of our behavior. Each nucleus can generate innumerable images, such as all the images of parents that have ever been shown in myth, art, or writing. Behind these, and never representable as such, are the parental archetypes of father and mother. These are inexhaustible in variety of images, yet each image is clearly identifiable as father and/or mother. Archetypes include many opposites nonrationally, such as positive and negative, material and spiritual. But whether they are the source of our images or of the basic organization of matter, we can call the patterning behind the effect an archetype. The archetype is rendered partially visible in material forms but remains unknowable in itself.

It is fundamental to the approach taken here that the archetypes assert what may be called their unity or simplicity in each manifestation. A very simple and concrete example is the healing of a cut finger in which the wrinkle in the skin which was cut is reproduced in the healing, as if there were a unified image of the whole finger to work from, complete with wrinkle. The fact that small whole numbers maintain their integrity in the evolution of an organism comprised of trillions of cells is another example (two legs, two eyes, five fingers, one nose with two nostrils, etc.). We may therefore seek to find the causes of this remarkable fact in the nature of the matter out of which human consciousness has evolved, and it would be unwise to omit such a search.

Small whole numbers, especially the first four, 1, 2, 3, and 4, have a tremendous psychological significance. This has been amply shown by Jung and von Franz. Of these, trinities and quaternities have been shown to be found in images of godhead, both in cultures and in the individual psyche. As part of the basis for consideration of images of the divine-human relationship, we will consider how these numbers 3 and 4 occur in the study of the "stuff of the universe" (Teilhard) from which we have evolved.

In attempting to grasp what this "stuff" is, which Teilhard also calls "spirit-matter," it is necessary to realize that our conceptualizations in some way depend upon the fact that we are trying to gain a conscious image or picture of something which is unconscious in any usual sense. Thus there is always the danger that we may be describing the nature of our consciousness more than the "objective entity." At the same time, we have some confidence that we *can* approach a description of that which is unconscious, simply because of the fact that our consciousness has indeed evolved from this spirit-matter.

We will find that the numbers 3 and 4 are strongly linked to the numbers of dimensions, forces, entities, properties, and symmetries (conservation laws) which must be considered by the physicist in the description of nature. After a few introductory paragraphs, these topics will be taken up in their order.

Any successful discussion of spirit-matter must begin with the fact of consciousness and its evolution within and out of that which is unconscious. Von Franz, in *Number and Time* (1974), and Teilhard, in *Human Energy*, have recognized this principle. Teilhard puts it as follows:

Instinctively, in their attempts to make an intellectual scheme of the universe, many try to use matter as their *starting point*. Because matter can be touched, and because it *appears* historically to have existed first, it is accepted without examination as the primordial stuff and most intelligible portion of the cosmos. But *this road leads nowhere*...Anyone who accepts this starting point blocks all roads that would bring one back to the present state of the universe. On the other hand, from a cosmos formed and made up of elementary 'freedoms,' it is easy to deduce...all the appearances of exactitude upon which the mathematical physics of matter is founded...There is neither spirit nor matter in the world; the 'stuff of the universe' is *spirit-matter*. No other substance than this could produce the human molecule. (Teilhard, 1969, pp. 23-24, 57-78)

On the one hand, we perceive and experience in terms of opposites. We know qualities only by contrast to their opposites or negatives. We could thus say that spirit and matter are our primary means of perceiving the world. They make up one primary pair of opposites by means of which we make a fundamental distinction about the nature of things. If this duality is *ours alone*, i.e., if it is not objective but wholly a part of our means of perceiving, then spirit and matter are a unity in a preperceptual background. They are inseparable *in* the objective reality.

On the other hand, if what we perceive as the distinctness of spirit and matter is at least somewhat objective, i.e., if our perceptive functions do not wholly deceive us as to the distinction between spirit and matter, we must *also* consider that there is a unitary preperceptual background in which they are one. This is true because we can establish the relatedness of spirit and matter just as well as we can the distinctness. This will be seen in the second section of this chapter, and elsewhere.

At this point also, we can make use of the guiding fact of the evolution of that which is conscious from that which is unconscious. Our whole perceptive system has evolved, as far as we can tell, from the primordial stuff of the universe: spirit-matter. Opposites have arisen in the form of conscious and unconscious, but this duality must be a potential of spirit-matter. That which is wholly unitary in itself cannot give rise to duality in a continuous evolutionary process. From this we can conclude that our perceived dualities are at least partly objective and not merely our way of perceiving things. We will return to this point on numerous occasions.

The second major introductory point to consider is the fact that our psychic processes, including all that is capable of being known and all our possible modes of organizing that knowledge, must be distinguished from the transpsychic, or psychoid, realities which lie behind the manifestations of *both* matter and spirit. We have grown up with the prejudice that while matter may be unknowable in itself, still spirit, at least as intellectual or conceptual functioning, is immediately experienced. While we are separate from matter, we identify with spirit. For example, Einstein's opinion was that "the laws of physics are free inventions of the human intellect." Nevertheless, since we know that our perception of matter at best only *approximates* the reality behind these perceptions, so, upon reflection, it is evident that our laws of physics are only approximate descriptions of that which governs the physical realm. While we can describe a star's behavior by certain well-known mathematical equations, it is obvious that a star does not solve any mathematical equations. It simply *is* in a patterned rather than chaotic form.

So it is also with other regularities in nature which we attempt to describe by means of physical "laws." We see that there is patterning, i.e., regular behavior, and we can describe these regularities mathematically with great, though not ultimate, precision. Two theories, such as Newton's laws and Einstein's relativity, may describe events with nearly equal precision while resting upon vastly different assumptions. All the while, we know that we are dealing with patterned behavior, even if we do not know whether our description is ultimately well founded.

It is equally evident that patterning is prior to the development of brains and of consciousness, for it *accounts* for the organizing of matter into brains and other organs. This patterning is what is here identified with spirit. Spirit has actual organizing power relative to the forms of entities and in their interrelations. More will be said on this topic later in this chapter.

The emergence of the modern notion of spirit-matter followed historically upon the demise of a purely mechanistic view of matter. The story of how this came about has often been told. The discovery of the reality of the uncertainty principle has made it impossible to predict the future from the present state of things because this principle states that we can never have sufficiently precise information about the present state. Moreover, the necessity of observation to obtain knowledge means that the act of observation perturbs the present state and thus *changes* the future. At the same time, it must be acknowledged that the conclusion that such a demise of the mechanistic view has truly occurred would be challenged by some reputable physicists, though the trend of acceptance is clear.

The demise follows upon three facts which, in turn, follow upon the central guiding fact mentioned earlier, namely that consciousness has evolved out of that which is unconscious. The three subdivisions are:

(1) The fact that physics is primarily conceptual, and only approximately mathematical. Observation of regularities in nature yields concepts. These concepts are hard-won and become refined over a lengthy period of time. An example is our modern concept of energy, which in Newton's time was called *vis viva* or living force. In the common understanding, energy is often still confused with force. But if we try to represent energy by the letter E and put it into a mathematical equation, we can't be certain that everything in the concept is present in the resulting solution of the equation.

(2) The fact that everyday concepts do not apply to the physical reality being described, except approximately and then only to objects of directly perceivable sizes, and under everyday sorts of conditions. Rather, we have *images* of things which are colored by the nature of our consciousness. We tend to leap to perceptions and later realize that we were not seeing well. Beyond that, even our best observations are shaped by the very means of observing, especially in microphysics and cosmology. Our concepts of things are also such tools or means of observing. In physics, for example, the nature of light is described in terms of waves and particles. We know what these are from everyday experience of things. Experiments show, however, that neither

of these concepts really applies to light. And yet they are the only concepts available (and properly so) for application to the description of such microphysical entities.

(3) The fact that, both conceptually and mathematically, contradiction is inherent in a complete description of physical situations, in all size ranges, from the microphysical to the cosmic. As was said above, macrophysical concepts such as wave and particle are the only ones we have for application to the microphysical realm, even though neither can apply. But the concepts of wave and particle are also contradictory *to each other*. This is a second level of contradiction. A third level is that between conscious and unconscious discussed in Chapter Four and between matter and spirit as such, discussed in the chapter and section on reality. In mathematics, Gödel proved that contradiction cannot be eliminated from mathematical systems as complicated as arithmetic and logic. In some cases the contradiction has been masked by an apparent precision. We have discovered in microphysics, for example, that it is a conceptual contradiction to try to set up simultaneous experiments to measure with extreme precision both the position and momentum of a body. In our ordinary world of relatively large objects, we *can* measure both of these with great precision. And yet we now realize that the same conceptual impossibility of doing so with absolute precision still applies.

That these three are facts which do indeed follow from the central guiding fact requires much substantiation. Still, it may be briefly said that it is so because conscious and unconscious, though formal contradictories, are obviously potentials of the evolving "stuff." Thus the evolution of consciousness from that which is unconscious becomes the *prime* example of the nonrational relatedness of contraries or opposites. This kind of relatedness of opposites is called *complementarity* in physics.

Small Whole Numbers and Physical Reality: The Number of Dimensions

One of the most central elements of experience relating to the numbers 3 and 4 is the set of "dimensions" called space and time. We commonly perceive space as three-dimensional and time as one-dimensional, which, taken together, make a four-dimensional "space-time continuum." Closely allied with this set is another parallel set called matter-energy. With these two sets we exhaust the fundamental terms of physical experience. In the case of the latter set, the manifestation of the numbers 3 and 4 is not so obvious, but it has been proposed that the second set (matter-energy) can be derived from the first (space-time). (See footnote 2, Chapter Five.)

Three spatial dimensions and one of time constitute the minimum dimensionality for the possibility of existence, if that word is to have palpable meaning. We might, for example, conceive of a flat world inhabited by flat beings, as was done in the famous book *Flatland* by Edwin Abbott (1952). Even this imagined world was three dimensional because time passed in it, but the point is that its two spatial dimensions constitute an impossibility, for actual zero thickness precludes matter as such. Matter, or mass, is inherently dependent upon volume, and even one atom's thickness already has volume, i.e., is not two dimensional or flat.

Along with the possibility for actualization, it is important to mention the ways of representing space, of dividing it, and defining a center. We will begin with two dimensions, for we are accustomed to representations on paper. Also, the fact that we live in a thin layer of atmosphere on the nearly two-dimensional surface of Earth has made the two-dimensional circle and cross especially significant as a symbol of the center. In our visualization of terrestrial space, we are more two-dimensional than three, for we greatly exaggerate the vertical and are quite unrealistic about it, as any pilot can testify.

A two-dimensional whole is a flat geometrical plane of infinite extension in all directions. We usually represent it by means of a circle or square, but the square already assumes some forward direction on the plane. Given, then, a two-dimensional whole, represented by a circle, O , one symmetrical division produces two halves, Φ . The agent of division is the line, which is the one-dimensional representation of a whole. Two symmetrical, orthogonal (right-angled) divisions produce four quarters *and* a center, $\oplus$.

For three spatial dimensions, the whole is represented by a sphere and the agent of division is the plane. A center and eight octants are produced by three divisions. In general, given an n-dimensional representation of a whole, the agent of division is an n–1 dimensional representation of a whole, and the nth symmetrical orthogonal division produces a center and 2^n parts.

In three dimensions we have the condition for matter met, namely volume, but we still lack sufficient conditions for existence. That which exists has *come into existence* via change, which requires time. Nothing is actualizable in space apart from time. Space-time is thus the minimum medium of existence, but, because of the characteristic of time that it "passes," it is not divisible in the same way as are the first three dimensions. The term *time* needs definition in a sense different from that in which any previous term needs definition. This is far from an easy task, but Kierkegaard has made an excellent start in *The Concept of Dread*[1] (1957).

Our usual notions of space and time are abstractions. Euclidean space, in which straight lines extend infinitely far without deviation, is pure fiction. Even our notions of non-Euclidean curved spaces are abstractions until we realize that it is *matter*, via gravity, which curves space. It is the great lesson of 20th-century cosmology that there is no space which is not the relationship of matter. The corresponding lesson with respect to time is that there is no time which is not the rhythm of matter, inherent in its *dynamis*. This fact has been amply brought out by von Franz in *Number and Time*.

While the 3 + 1 dimensionality of space-time is the *minimum* for actualization of existence, physicists have shown that it is also the *maximum* for there to be stability of orbits of planets around a sun. Thus this 3 + 1 dimensionality, as both minimum and maximum, is shown to be the case. Indeed, it is the only possible case of a world in which the gradual evolution of consciousness from that which is unconscious can occur.[2]

The fact that the 4 here appears as 3 + 1, and not as 2 + 2, provides a typical parallel to the psycholog-

---

1. See Appendix C for the full quotation.

2. This is not to say that there *aren't* other dimensions but that ordinarily we do not contact them. Physically, we are pretty safely confined to our world of one temporal and three spatial dimensions. As early as 1884 Edwin Abbott, in *Flatland* (1952, p. 92), suggested that once the bounds of a single dimension have been

ical phenomena, for which this is often the case. Yet it is not the only such example from physics, as will be seen in all of the succeeding sections.

THE NUMBER OF FORCES

Physicists have discovered four basic forces at work in the cosmos: gravitational, electromagnetic, "weak" nuclear, and "strong" nuclear, in increasing order of strength of interaction. If the strong nuclear force is arbitrarily assigned a strength of 1.0, the relative strengths of the forces would be:

strong nuclear	– 1.0
electromagnetic	– 0.01
weak nuclear	– 0.0001
gravitational	
–0.000000000000000000000000000000000000001	

The three strongest forces then are not so very different in strength, but the weakest is weaker by many orders of magnitude.

The three strongest forces are also fundamentally different in *nature* from gravity in that they are "shielded" forces. This means that if other matter intervenes between the acting particle and its potential object, the intervening matter shields the object from the force. By contrast, in the case of gravity every particle in the cosmos acts upon (attracts) every

---

breached, there is, mathematically speaking, no reason to stop at three or four. Independently, I printed a little paper in 1969 for my astronomy classes in which I suggested that thinking about "black holes" would enable us eventually to visualize additional spatial dimensions. By now the cosmological literature is full of such references, sparked and led by the work of the most eminent living cosmologist, John Archibald Wheeler. But we *live and have evolved* in a stable four-dimensional system.

other particle in the cosmos, regardless of distance or the presence of intervening matter.

The three relatively strong shielded forces are also grouped together and separated from gravity by the fact that in their case the force between identical particles is repulsive, whereas for gravity it is attractive. On three counts, therefore, the four forces are divided into 3 + 1: three being strong and local, and the fourth being weak but cosmic.

Gravity, therefore, is the only candidate for the force which unifies the cosmos. In fact, its cumulative effect can enable it to dominate the other three even in small regions of space, as in the case of a "dying" star which becomes a black hole when the mutual gravitational attraction of its constituent particles overpowers the tremendous pressures of densities up to a billion tons per cubic centimeter. A fuller description of how this comes about would be out of place here.

In spite of the diverse character of these forces, many physicists now believe that they are but different manifestations of a single "unified field" force called supergravity. The diagram below (adapted from Freedman and van Nieuwenhuizen, 1978) shows the stages of this unification which is still tentative in one area. But it is seen that even in their unification the four known forces show the grouping of three and one.

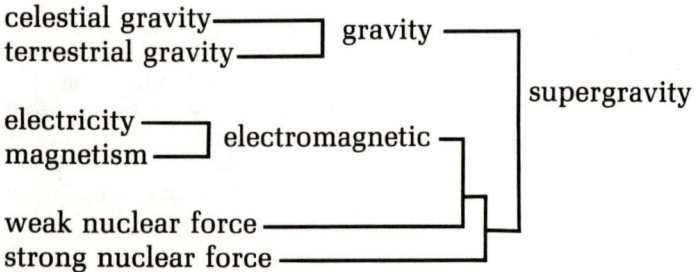

Two of these forces, gravity and electromagnetic, show early unifications of apparent dualities. In the case of electromagnetism, it seemed for a long while that electricity and magnetism governed quite distinct phenomena. In the case of gravity, the apparent duality was more psychologically based, namely upon the assumption that things on the Earth must follow different laws from things in the celestial regions where all was "quintessential." Thus, Newton's unification of terrestrial and celestial gravity, by showing that the moon follows the same law as the falling apple, was filled with deep psychological and religious impact.

The Number of Fundamental Entities/Quantities

A physics course usually begins with the various systems of units of measurement, e.g., the MKS system with its three fundamental quantities of length, mass, and time, with their units, the meter (M), the kilogram (K), and the second (S), respectively. With these we can begin to derive other quantities such as force, energy, and temperature, though some say that temperature is also fundamental. Later on, in the second or third physics course, the idea of electric charge is introduced as a fourth really fundamental quantity, though some physicists like to derive it also from the others. Nonetheless, mass, length, time, and electric charge have much common acceptance as a basis for classical physics. These fundamental quantities are sometimes called fundamental "dimensions," so that the concept of dimension is expanded beyond those of space and time alone.

In addition to fundamental quantities, we have fundamental entities. If we stay at a practical level and don't look too deeply, we might truly say that we can account for all matter in terms of four such particles: the proton, the neutron, the electron, and the highly elusive neutrino—again a natural grouping of 3 + 1.[3] The photon is a special case, of a kind different from these four. Rather than being an entity in its own right, it is an "exchange" particle, one of a class of such exchange particles which account for the interactions of the entities. It all begins to get rather complex, but always we see these groupings in fours with the 3 + 1 arrangement. This is the pattern to notice as we proceed.

Then there are the "constants of nature" such as the speed of light, the universal constant of gravitation, the constant of electrical interaction, and Planck's constant (the universal constant of action in the quantum theory). So we have dimensions, forces, fundamental quantities, fundamental entities, and constants of nature. These are all interrelated in extremely intricate ways. We would like to find the most solid basis for saying that the numbers 3 and 4 appear as strongly as they do. We find, however, that we must rely upon common usage, for there is no absolute basis.

Every attempt to find an absolute basis for the choice of fundamental quantities must fail, for by arbitrary choices of values and "dimensions" of the constants of nature it is possible to reduce the number of such quantities even to zero. For example, relativists tell us that it is more "natural" to measure time in meters, using light travel time to set the stan-

---

3. The electron is lighter in mass than the proton and the neutron by a factor of almost 2000, but no one is yet certain that the neutrino has a mass of its own. There are some indirect, unconfirmed indications that the neutrino may have a mass of 1/25,000 of that of the electron. It seems to have some characteristics of a particle, namely a similar quantity of "spin," but it remains enigmatic in respect to mass. Even so, the *existence* of several types of neutrino has been experimentally confirmed.

dard. Here *natural* means "in tune with the fundamental nature of the construction of the physical cosmos." Mathematical physicists say it is more natural because the dimension of time appears in mathematical equations on the same footing as the dimensions of space. The interval between events can appear sometimes to be space-like and sometimes time-like, but all four dimensions appear in all cases. Why not, if all are equal, measure time in meters or light-meters? We also are used to something similar when we describe astronomical distances in light-years. If we can get rid of the second of time in meters or light-meters, we have reduced the number of fundamental quantities.

John A. Wheeler, a leading cosmologist, has given another rationale for the absorption of time into spacelike thinking. He uses the fact that the speed of light is a *constant* to interpret that speed as a conversion factor between meters and seconds, similar to the conversion factor of 5280 feet per mile. If we multiply some given number of miles by 5280, we get the equivalent distance in feet. The speed of light is 299,792,500 meters per second. If we multiply a given number of seconds by this factor, we get the equivalent in meters of light travel time. He says that in physics:

> The conversion between seconds and meters, namely the speed of light, c = 299,792,500 meters per second, was regarded as a sacred number. It was not recognized as a mere conversion factor like the factor of conversion between miles and meters—a factor that arose out of historical accidents alone, with no deeper physical significance. (Taylor and Wheeler, 1966, p. 2.)

For most of us, the natural means of measuring time is with clocks, which differ in obvious ways from meter sticks, and it is easier to say "Just a minute" than to say "just eighteen billion meters." In our natural way of perceiving the world, there *are* fundamental quantities and also constants of nature which take on various numerical values in different systems of units.

Because it is unsatisfactory to reduce the number of fundamental quantities to zero, our task is to employ other criteria in discovering how many such quantities there are. These are clarity, simplicity, meaning, common usage, and symmetry. If possible, the quantities chosen should also yield the easiest means of measurement and of comparison with a fundamental standard, but in this area lie many well-known conflicts. Here our choice is for the priority of symmetry rather than for simplicity of measurement. Since every symmetry in physics entails a conservation law (such as the law of conservation of matter or energy) and vice versa, we really are saying that conservation laws will take precedence.

In what follows immediately, an understanding of the terms presented is not the object and is in fact unnecessary. But as we work our way to the striking diagram of groupings of seven fundamental quantities in threes and fours, it seems necessary to lay some basis, which the reader may, however, prefer to skip over, moving directly to the diagram itself.

Often we see pairs or quaternities of quantities grouped around the universal constants by means of the fundamental *principles* of physics, e.g., the principle of the conservation of energy, the principle of the conservation of momentum, the principle of the universality of invariants, and the famous uncertainty principle.[4]

---

4. As an example of the fact that physicists *do* so group quantities symbolically in threes and fours, we may take the following diagram, adapted from *Spacetime Physics*, by Taylor and

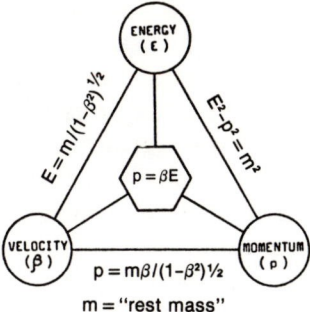

$$m = \text{``rest mass''}$$

By means of the uncertainty principle, the quantities of space, time, energy, and momentum are gathered around Planck's constant (h). These four quantities are related by pairs in different ways.

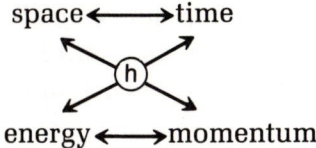

Space and momentum are related: the uncertainty in the position and the uncertainty in the momentum of an object, multiplied together, can never be less than Planck's constant. The same is true of the uncertainty in the energy of an object, and the uncertainty in the time at which it possesses that energy. But space is also related to time symmetrically and energy is related to momentum, since they are both subjects of conservation laws regarding symmetries of matter in space and time.

By means of the principle of the universality of in-

Wheeler (1966, p. 120). It is not necessary to "understand" the quantities and the formulas which relate them, but only to observe the fact that the interrelationships are presented diagrammatically by the authors.

variants, other quantities are gathered to the constant speed of light (c). These are mentioned here only for the sake of the visual effect of the following diagram which shows groupings of three and four. The central tetrahedron grouping relates the "invariants," mass and velocity, to the variants, energy and momentum. These two variants then form a square with two other variants, space and time, around Planck's constant (h), as in the diagram above, while the two invariants form a triangle with the single space-time invariant, the "interval," around the velocity of light. Altogether we have a web of quantities and constants which unites the microphysical world to the cosmos. Again, nothing is proven in the diagram but that these groupings naturally occur and impress physicists with their meaning. All of this is but a small sampling of the ways in which small whole numbers, and especially the numbers three and four, stand out in physics.

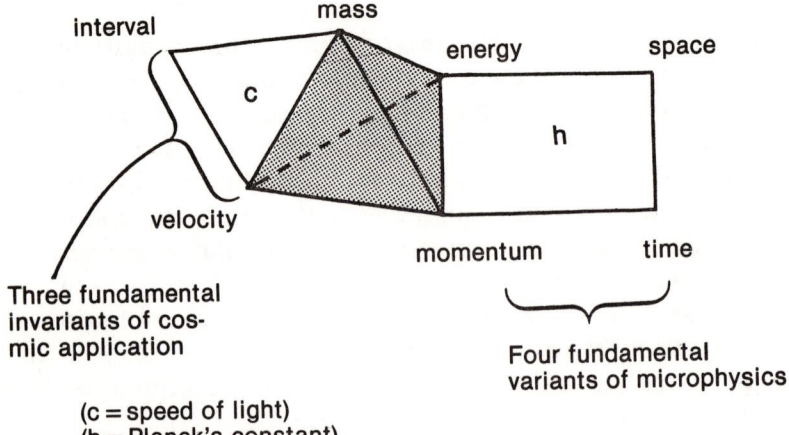

Figure 4. Groupings of Three and Four

Spirit as Patterning in Evolution

Spirit is here taken as patterning, including the dynamism by means of which patterns "take shape." We attempt to *describe* this patterning by means of, say, laws of physics, or classifications of forms, but the patterns themselves simply exist. A star, for example, does not *solve* any mathematical equations in taking a spherical form or in producing nuclear energy. The equations which mathematical physicists use to describe the behavior of stars are merely a means of "getting at" the regularities in natural processes which are nonperceptual or preperceptual in themselves. We have here an analogy with symbols, behind which lie a nonperceptual, nonrational "something" whose manifestation or representation the symbol is. To many physicists, especially the greatest, it seems a pure miracle that mathematics applies to the physical world at all.

At any rate, this patterning/dynamism is the case. To demonstrate that it should be *this* that is termed spirit would make this chapter quite long, but it is hoped that reflection upon it will uncover its striking aptitude to the reader. (See Chapter Two.)

To say that pattern is inseparable from matter would then be to say that there is no matter without spirit. But the nature of the patterning can be shown to be quite remarkable, naturally leading to the question of whether there can be spirit apart from matter. Let us therefore look at the simplest form of spirit-matter, the hydrogen atom.

Pictures of representations of the various forms which a hydrogen atom can assume according to its mathematical model are shown in Figure 5. These are not pictures of hydrogen atoms. In the center of each "picture" a small dot has been placed to repre-

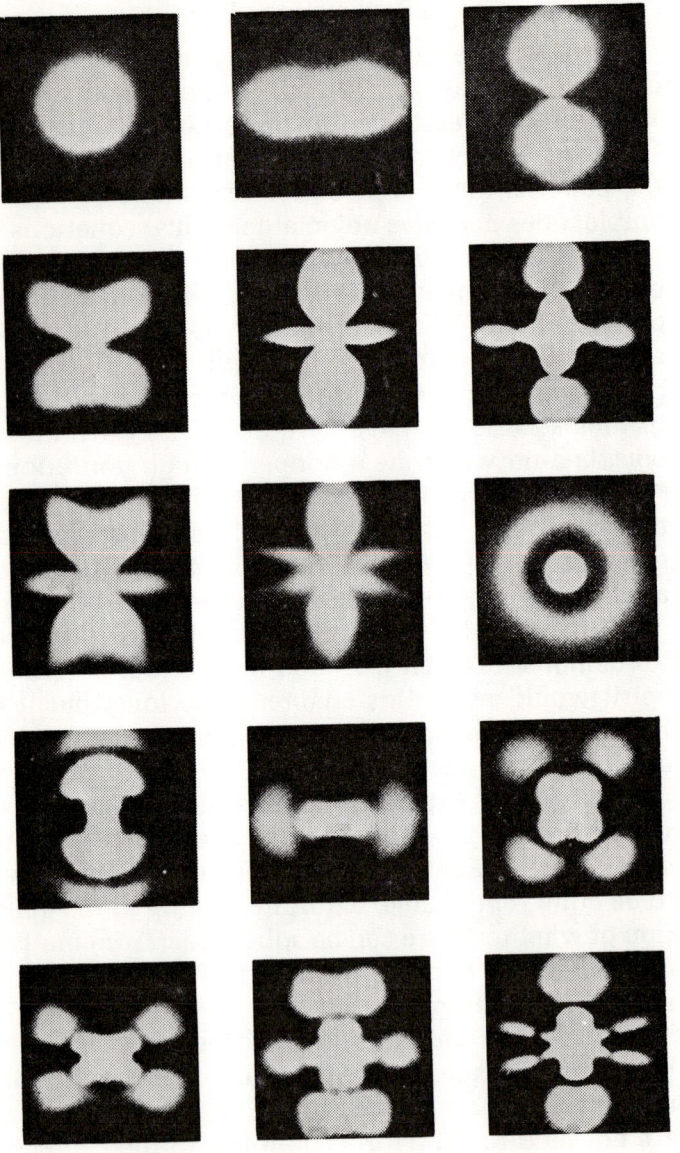

Figure 5. Forms of Hydrogen Atoms

Harvey E. White. Pictorial representations of the electron cloud for hydrogen-like atoms. *Physical Review* (1931) 37:1423.

sent the proton which comprises the nucleus of each atom. The fuzzy image which fills most of each frame represents a possible configuration for the single electron which, together with the proton, makes up the atom itself. In each frame is a *single* electron, though the image appears to have several parts. Each of the single- or multi-lobed images is an example of what physicists call a "probability distribution" or "probability cloud," meaning that where the cloud is thickest, the electron is most likely to be "found."

But it is well known that an electron, when found, changes an aspect of its nature. When traveling it is a wave, but when it interacts, i.e., is found, it is a particle. (The same is true of a photon of light.) It is also known that it is meaningless to describe the shapes in the pictures as clouds in which an electron is traveling as a particle. Such a description would violate one of the very foundations of the quantum theory, namely the uncertainty principle. We have begun to learn to avoid "electron existence" language, that is, the use of words which in itself assumes that the electron *does* exist as something resembling a hard, round little thing. An example is the question, "Where can we find *the electron* in the probability cloud?" If the probability cloud *is* the electron, then we cannot expect to find the electron *in* the cloud. When we "find" the electron in such a way that it registers on an instrument as being in a specific location, it is no longer that cloud. Our understanding of this point has developed gradually. In the early parts of the century, we thought of electrons as those hard little objects in definite circular or elliptical orbits. Later we said that the orbit is unknown but that the electron is somewhere inside the cloud. Now our understanding of the nature of chemical bonds and their physical strength, say, to resist bending, forces us to view the cloud as the electron itself, in *one* of its complementary manifestations (wave), the *other* of which is a particle.

Thus each picture represents all that we can know of the shape and location of the electron in the particular state shown. To say that what the picture represents is the electron itself is no error. *It is a cloud of matter*, but not an amorphous cloud. Rather, it is highly patterned, with an extensive repertoire of patterns. If spirit is what is behind the observed patterning, then these pictures give us a remarkable model for the inseparability of spirit and matter. This cloud has mass or substance, yet the pattern is intrinsic and is not merely manifest in the interrelationships of particles.

The fuzziness of the pictures also indicates that there is no sharp boundary to an electron. In fact, there is no boundary at all unless it is the finitude of the cosmos—as Teilhard said (*Phenomenon of Man*, p. 45), each atom is coextensive with the universe. This was not and is not mere philosophical speculation. The mathematical physicists know that locations at great distances from where most of the electron is have relevance in at least two ways. First, the clouds *are* fuzzy, and the mathematical descriptions of them are well defined and still finite, though very small at great distances. This means that an infinitesimal part of every electron is spread throughout the cosmos. Secondly, in the process of obtaining mathematical descriptions of localized electrons, certain mathematical terms which would otherwise "blow up at infinity" must be arbitrarily eliminated. This point is also discussed in a different way in Chapter Four and Appendix A where the characteristics of "waves" and particles are given. What is meant here is that solutions are found in applying

Schrödinger's equation, which is known to be very effective in describing "matter-waves," but these solutions contain more than is physically usable. Some parts must simply be crossed out, and the remaining parts are employed for the accurate description.

So each particle is not only coextensive with the cosmos, but is therefore also coextensive with all other particles in the cosmos, although *this* particle is mostly here and *that* particle is mostly there. Thus the notion of action at a distance must be re-examined, for nothing is really separated from anything else. This idea is similar to that in Einstein's general theory of relativity, in which each particle curves the space where it is, even extending slight "gravitational" effects to the most distant part of the cosmos.[5]

Again, hydrogen is the very *simplest* form of spirit-matter. In stars, by means of nuclear processes, hydrogen atoms fuse into more and more complex chemical elements. In the whole life of a star, the full range of elements is produced from hydrogen and helium to uranium and beyond. The chemical elements out of which our earth and its living beings are made were produced in stars, particularly in stellar explosions which recycled this material into cosmic space, to mix there with primordial hydrogen and then form into new stars with planets.

---

5. It may turn out that gravitation (curvature of space) is "simply" the *presence* of each particle in other parts of the cosmos. Ideas along this line were presented many years ago by J. A. Wheeler in his *Geometrodynamics,* in which he says:

This subject can be considered to date from the period 1955-1957 when it was discovered that mass and electricity can be fashioned out of curved empty space (Wheeler, 1962, p. xi).

The first step of complexification is thus the building of all other elements from hydrogen. Under less violent conditions than those of stellar explosions or stellar interiors, these elements combine chemically, first into inorganic compounds, then into organic compounds, life molecules, and finally into living organisms. Thus we desire to see the nature of the continuity of the evolutionary process, looking at it from the point of view of the perpetuation of patterns. An excellent example is the step from elemental hydrogen to the role of hydrogen in a particular crystalline form of water, the snowflake (Figure 6).

If we compare a snowflake with a six-lobed hydrogen atom picture (Figure 5), it may not be too much of a leap to see the relationship of shapes. In the snowflake, the six-lobed pattern takes preponderance. In other patterns of nature, other numbers predominate. Weisskopf has stated clearly and beautifully the relationship of symmetries in nature to those in the hydrogen atom pictures:

> The patterns of [the figure] and their inherent symmetries determine the behavior of the atoms; they are the basis of the orderly arrangement in molecules and also of the symmetric arrangement of atoms or molecules in crystals. The simple beauty of a crystal reflects on a larger scale the fundamental shapes of the atomic patterns. Ultimately the regularities of form and structure that we see in nature, ranging from the hexagonal shape of a snowflake to the intricate symmetries of living forms in flowers and animals, are based upon the symmetries of these atomic patterns. (Weisskopf, 1979, p. 109)

Again, in complexification, the relatively small number—in the hundreds—of realized hydrogen atom patterns yields an almost infinite variety of snowflake patterns while retaining a basic geometry

Figure 6. Snowflakes
(Bentley and Humphreys, 1962, pp. 70, 116, 129, 186)

in which small whole numbers still are visible, in this case the number six.

A point to note carefully here is that as water molecules freeze onto the outer end of one arm of the flake, molecules freezing onto another arm somehow "know" how to freeze in precise symmetry with the first, though the distance between the two events is large compared to the size of the molecule. This could be the case only if there is an "image" being symmetrically extended as the snowflake grows, or rather not an image but a *pattern* behind the highly individualized snowflake image which we see. This pattern cannot depend only upon nearby molecules. Since the crystal has the ability to correct for minor "freezing errors" and to continue with the original pattern, there must be some degree of dependence upon the whole flake.

Edmund Sinnott in *The Biology of the Spirit* presents several examples of the next stage: the *mobility* of the wholeness pattern. Just as the snowflake exhibits the wholeness pattern with its ability to move water molecules into position and to overcome minor freezing errors, the pine tree shows the potential of the pattern for restoration through movement. Here is an example:

> A pine tree is as simple an organism as one can find, save among the lowliest of living things. It has few of the complexities of an animal—no stomach, no heart, no muscles, no nerves, no sense organs, and certainly no brain. Despite this, it possesses a bodily pattern to which it stubbornly adheres, maltreat it as you will...
> First, bind a cluster of growing terminal branches with a loop around the whole about halfway down, so that the umbrella cannot fully open. Though the lower portions of each branch are thus held vertical, the free upper portions act like

> typical branches and spread out until they reach
> the normal angle of about seventy degrees to the
> main axis or trunk. They have come as close as
> they can to restoring the typical growth pattern of
> the tree. (Sinnott, 1955, pp. 18-19)

The same mobility of the wholeness pattern is evident in the healing of wounds on a tree as the wood flows over cut places over a period of years, and also in the much more efficient healing processes in the animal realm. So far, we see the development of the healing symbol in terms of processes going on in *individuals,* in snowflakes, pine trees, and physical wounds of animals. Ultimately, as people move in social situations for healing of psychological wounds, this mobility is maximized and its significance extended *beyond* individuals. Even more important is the fact that the perception of the wound or malady in the social fabric of humanity becomes conscious, and the movement toward healing becomes choiceful, even when it involves sacrifice.

Since some of the snowflake patterns form pinelike needles, it seemed appropriate to employ the pine for this intermediate stage, but we were following the number six.

Another six-lobed development much further along the evolutionary line is the brain (Figure 7). The cerebrum of the brain is divided medically into eight lobes, two each (left and right) for each of the major divisions (called frontal, parietal, occipital, and temporal). But the central *cross-sections* shown in Figure 7 display the aspect of six-lobedness, both vertically and horizontally. Here we are concerned with the *visual* facts. The correlation of the visual appearance with medical definitions would require a lengthy explanation. Somehow the sixness remains, though now incomparably more molecules are involved, and incomparably more complex molecules than in the case of snowflakes. This recalls the original sixness of certain hydrogen atom configurations.

An analogy to the complexification process being described may be seen in the photographic science of holography. A hologram records three-dimensional information in a two-dimensional plane on a photographic plate or film. By illuminating the hologram with laser light, one can reconstruct a three-dimensional visual image, including the ability to look "behind" foreground objects to see what is in the background. But the remarkable feature of holograms, analogous to the complexification process, is that if one cuts or breaks off half, or a quarter, or even a very small piece of the film or plate, one can still reconstruct the *entire* scene which was holographed, but the smaller the piece the less detail, and the more depth of field.

We have then the possibility that the sixness of the brain is the same sixness of the hydrogen atom, but with the *detail* filled in. Certainly we must say that the complex molecular interactions of living organisms are all potentials inherent in hydrogen atoms, for these substances evolved from hydrogen atoms. The pattern is there to be fulfilled in detail when more delicate environments allow for the evolution of more complex entities. But the pattern is present at all times, from the very beginning.

The consideration of the evolutionary development of brains yields another remarkable insight. The squirrel has a brain shaped like ours, though it does not include the function of reflexive verbal thought. Nonetheless, we may say of the squirrel's brain (from hindsight) that it is the *kind* of organ which will develop capability for thought through

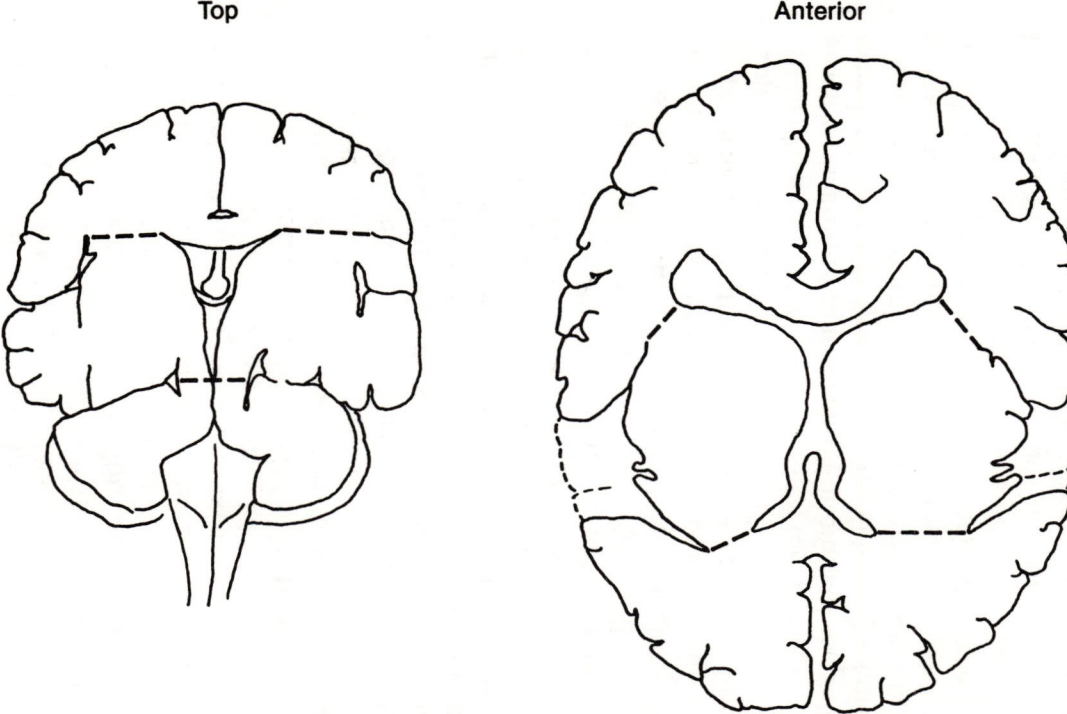

Figure 7. The Brain: Vertical and Horizontal Cross-Sections

evolution. We can say that it is the kind of organ whose *entelechy* is conscious thought.

Thought is only an example. Who knows what functions are in the process of organic development of spirit-matter *now*, to be enlivened in our successors? Nevertheless, potentialities limit and guide —or pattern—things, as well as enable their development. We can say that an organic development shows entelechy when the organ exists prior to the function which is its evolutionary goal and is headed in that direction by means of prior potentialities.

Our analogy may now be used to look back to hydrogen atoms for other archetypal images, particularly the Self. In some sense the hydrogen atom, in the inseparability of its spirit and matter aspects, in its simplicity and complexity, in its relation to small whole numbers (and in other ways), is an image of the Self, i.e., a material reflection of God.

As in a hologram, as the picture grows, i.e., as spirit-matter complexifies, the image becomes more clear and more differentiated. It produces all living forms, and especially the human form, singled out because of the enlivening of conscious thought in its brain. But the human body is not merely a life-support system for the brain.

It is known that organs outside the brain pre-process the stimuli that reach the brain, but the full extent of the participation of the body in psychic processes is certainly not known. Here we may perhaps take a clue from human God-images, which have been geometric, vegetative (especially as tree or flower), animal-like, and anthropomorphic. In the latter case, the God-image is not that of a disembodied brain but of the whole person, or of a dual male-female person. Following Teilhard, we may also speak of a totality of persons as included, but this has sometimes also implied the human form as the form of the whole. Perhaps the human body as a whole is the organ of the Self, in which case the analogy is enhanced by the inclusion of both conscious and the unconscious within it.

At some point (evolutionarily speaking, a "point" might encompass thousands of years), the Self would be ready to be enlivened, to fulfill its function in relation to consciousness, to begin functioning according to its entelechy. The spirit which oversaw the development of the Self over the eons can now "enter," can give its gift to, or of, consciousness. Humans can now be conscious of the spirit's immanent activity. The Self always was *inside* the body as potentiality, continually being projected onto outer objects which carried its value. As its function is fulfilled, we feel it to be *entered* by spirit. It is not a case, as Teilhard says, of matter becoming spirit, but rather of spirit-matter gradually fulfilling more and more of its potential. One might be tempted to say its *spiritual* potential, but one must be careful to keep the balance: spirit is fulfilled in matter.

We must always be aware of both sides of the affirmation that there is no matter without spirit and no spirit without matter. It has seemed that there are two aspects of spirit: one in the process of emergence within complexification of organic forms, and one seeming to descend into matter from a source beyond. Isn't this latter spirit without matter? Is not God, at least, conceived as apart from matter? Or, what might be the corresponding matter?

It may be the cosmos as a whole. Upon reflection, this is the obvious place to look. The spirit descending seems to come from an infinite sea of potentiality, but this is also and always the potentiality of organic interconnections inherent in the tiniest material particles. It comes out of a *totality*, and the cosmos is such a totality. The implication is that not only the material in one's immediate vicinity is effective in shaping local interconnections, but also that which is at a distance, which is a sort of psychological Mach's principle.[6] This concept also adds meaning to the well-known ancient paradox that the center and periphery are one. Thus we return, in the end, to the totality whose image is both the whole and the simplest atom within the whole, and have seen how both end and beginning can shape the middle, in which we reside.

---

6. Mach hypothesized that the inertia of local bodies is dependent upon the total mass distribution in the cosmos.

6
Holographic Evolution

The earth brings forth fruit of herself.
Jesus of Nazareth, Mark 4:28

In the previous chapter a rough outline of holographic evolution was given by means of three sets of patterns: those of atoms, snowflakes, and brains. The purpose of the present chapter is to fill in details and bring out implications. This will be done by considering how several central aspects of human life—love, freedom, consciousness, and meaning—may possibly be derived from physical properties by complexification.

LOVE

It may seem strange to begin with love, but the reason will soon be apparent. The universality of love (in its greater forms) as the driving force of human activity can be compared only to the universality of gravity as the driving force of the physical evolution of the cosmos.

Gravity separates the primordial matter into distinct centers: first into galaxies, then into stars. It would be impossible to develop human entities without first dividing the cosmos into manageable hunks. But having made this separation, gravity compresses each star-to-be so that it begins to complexify matter into the full range of chemical elements. Note that gravity is a purely attractive force: every particle in the universe is attracted to every other. But this force, the subtlest and most pervasive force in the universe, is able both to unite and separate by means of attractive pulls in opposite directions. With regard to a *whole*, it can only unite, but it can separate *parts* of a whole from each other. The analogy of gravity with love, which I want to draw, is thus deepened. Gravity is the root of all of the physical dynamism in the universe.

In Chapter Five it was seen that the other forces, which are much stronger than gravity but not all-pervasive, are now viewed by many as offshoots, along with gravity, of a still more universal force called "supergravity." The name seems significant in that the three stronger forces were not chosen for the name of the more universal force. Indeed, the three- —electrical, weak nuclear and strong nuclear—all exhibit a shieldedness which prevents them from being unifiers of the cosmos. Yet they are extremely important in the way things work. It should be noted that electrical attraction[1] and repulsion are highly sym-

---

1. I use the electrical force rather than the nuclear force in this analogy because that is the force responsible for visible forms via the structural stability of matter and via chemistry (the interaction of electron patterns in atoms). The more powerful forces are responsible for the *variety* of chemical elements at a much deeper, more primitive stage , when the primal complexification occurs in stars.

bolic in human relations, yet are not the same as gravity. Love—as complexified gravity in the analogy—is often overpowered by less subtle attractions and repulsions, such as blind "falling in love" or equally blind sudden hate. But though the lesser attractions share the name *love* in English, the love which is analogous to gravity remains present as a subtle unification of everything human. In spite of the many apparent divisions among peoples in today's world, some individuals are gaining planetary consciousness and intuiting that which unifies all people. Perhaps it is more effective because there is now a greater mass of humanity than ever before (as Teilhard thought), or because some individuals have become more human.

In physics every event in which matter comes together under an attractive force generates energy. The poetic quotation which began Chapter Two states this principle in psychological terms, but it is good physics as well. The general coming together of matter in stars releases the energy which heats them to incandescence, and thus also generates the internal pressure which gives them *duration*. As the material gathers more closely and gravity increases due to this proximity, the release of gravitational energy raises the temperature to the point at which nuclear processes occur and complexification of hydrogen into heavier elements begins. In each subsequent stage of stellar evolution there is a net *contraction*.

One of the most important of these stages is a centration at the very end of the life of certain massive stars in which gravity squeezes the electrons of each atom into the nucleus of the atom. This happens suddenly in a large region of the core of the star, resulting in an almost instantaneous loss of support.

The electrons had heretofore played a major role in providing pressure to support the outer layers of the star, but now they have merged into the nuclei. The ensuing collapse is a centration so powerful that the energy released in the process blows away the outer half of the star. Simultaneously, by means of the extreme temperatures produced, it converts the matter blown away into the full range of chemical elements.

This is one form of supernova explosion. It is of extreme importance to us because the very atoms of which our Earth and our bodies are made were produced in such an explosion. We literally *are* stardust. Later, this stardust mixes with primordial hydrogen remaining in the galaxy. Then, when a new star forms, it already contains heavy elements out of which planets are made. Planets provide a cooler, more gentle, environment in which evolution can proceed to develop forms of greater complexity.

Gravity drives this whole process, even its moments of extreme violence. *Gravity* is our name for an ultimate fact of relationship. It produces *energy* which is our name for dynamic interchange.

The temperature which would be sufficient to disrupt an entity or a process is a key to thinking about the process of complexification. For example, atomic nuclei are so stable that it would take temperatures on the order of 100,000,000,000°C to break them apart. At the same time, the number of different kinds of atomic nuclei is very small. There are around 100 elements, each with several nuclear varieties, for a total of around 500.

The next step in the ladder of complexification is related to the amount of energy with which atomic nuclei hold onto their electrons in forming whole atoms. Temperatures of thousands to millions of degrees are needed to strip the electrons away from the nuclei, so we can see that much less energy is involved in maintaining the electron envelope of atoms than in the building of the nuclei.

Temperatures of around 1,000°C will break down most inorganic chemical compounds. There are many thousands of such compounds, so we have here an increase of complexification, with a corresponding delicacy of bonding. When we move in complexity from inorganic chemical compounds to the simpler organic compounds, the number sky-rockets, again with a corresponding decrease in the energy with which the elements are bonded together. This is shown by the fact that temperatures of several hundred degrees suffice to break down most of them. For example, most of us have heated sugar to watch it turn to carbon with the liberation of water.

The temperature range from 0°C to 100°C is, of course, that in which water is in liquid form (at standard atmospheric pressure on the earth), and is the range in which active life and evolution occur. The number of different life-molecules is boundless, because they can form almost endless chains with different internal sequences, and actually do so in our DNA molecules. Very few living organisms can withstand temperatures of 100°C (boiling) for long, which is why boiling is so effective in purification. The more complex living entities can stand much less, especially while remaining active. Some animals can hibernate at lower temperatures and some can remain active over a fairly wide range of body temperature, but our own range of body temperature for health and activity is a very narrow one, around 37°C (98.6°F). We know that if the temperature rises more than 3 or 4 degrees C, delirium occurs and life shortly ends unless the temperature is reduced. At the same time, the complexity is enormous. In *Intelligent Life in the Universe*, Carl Sagan tells us that to print the information in a human DNA molecule would take 133 volumes the size of an unabridged dictionary. Then the number of possible different DNA molecules of the size of human DNA would equal the number of possible different 133 volume *sets* of books of that size. Any change, even the smallest such as the exchange of two single letters, would constitute a difference. Even if one considers the number of different *meaningful* 133-volume sets of such books, it is absolutely staggering to contemplate. Again, as the energy involved in each interconnection decreases, the number of possible interconnections rises vastly.

It has been argued above in various ways that evolution is proceeding as a process of spiritualization in so far that it actualizes new potentials of the Patterning. Now we take a step from hard physics, but a step indicated by that evolutionary direction. If thought is one of the intermediate ends of that process, what can we say of the physical conditions under which thought flourishes? Jung suggested *analogies* of psychic and physical energies, but it is also certain that the energy used for thought by living humans requires the *conversion* of physical energy to intensity of thought or contemplation. This is, in itself, a form of spiritualization of the physical.

It takes a fairly stable, comfortable environment (when seen against the range of temperatures in the cosmos) for thought to function. The energy of the interconnection of *thoughts* must be much less than that of the molecular bonds in DNA. Thought is much more easily disrupted, but its numerical possibilities must exceed the number of different meaningful human DNA molecules by a tremendous factor.

It is interesting to note that concentration by means of meditation lowers the energy level of the body, gets it "out of the way." It also brings the mind to a point of calm, brings its "temperature" to a minimum. This is one means of increased perception of ripples from the patterning.

To return to the possibility of love as a complexified form of the simple physical bonds, we are looking for a force which is cohesive and relatively weak. Of human attractions, the ones which we are most apt to call the deepest love are indeed the most subtle and yet somehow the most pervasive. The word *inclusiveness* or even *all-inclusiveness* expresses this quality. Even as lesser attractions and repulsions give us strong pushes and pulls, beneath all such forces is a steady inclusion, if only it can be perceived. In physics, the inclusive principle *par excellence* is gravity. It unifies the cosmos and is not turned off in situations wherein stronger forces dominate, but operates as a steady background. It may even be that love is not *complexified* gravity but the effect of gravity itself operating in complexified matter. If the analogy holds, it even brings about the situations in which the stronger but less universal forces become active.[2]

As we become more highly complexified, it may well be that we develop increased potential sensitivi-

---

2. This idea has two thrusts. One is that all of the forces of nature are brought into play in response to gravity in the evolution of the cosmos. The other is related to the fact that the four forces possibly may be derived from "supergravity." In *Geometrodynamics* (1962, p. xi), J. A. Wheeler states that matter and electricity can be constructed out of "curved empty space," which suggests that nuclear and electrical forces are derived from a form of gravity which produces space-curvature on a small scale, as gravity does on a large scale.

ty in the perception of the forces tending to manifest the Patterning in its complexity and universality. It is interesting to note that physicists are now making great efforts to discover how to perceive gravitational events. For us to perceive the universality inwardly requires sensitivity and careful listening. The great humans among us generally are seen as great to the degree that they have developed this talent. As more of us listen for this aspect of the patterning, we may find that its centrative power will more easily dominate those psychic forces whose individual bonds are inherently so much stronger. In other words, we will respond to the cosmos rather than being dominated by our individual psychic urges. Just as without a wound there is nothing to heal, no substance to heal, so also without diversity there is nothing to unite. The establishment first of cultures and then of individuals within cultures seems to have been the thrust of evolution so far, and this process is far from complete even now. The beauties of individual humans and of their cultures enrich the earth beyond imagining, but will enrich it much more fully as the world becomes one.

The interplay of all the forces is clearly necessary in a complete description of the total patterning, but it seems much too early in the perceptive process to specify the trends of the balance of love with respect to the bivalent forces. The work of individuals in establishing ever wider frames of reference for their actions seems to hold much promise in this area. It takes much work to sense the deeper desire of that which most wants fulfillment in the cosmos and to align one's efforts toward its fulfillment, sacrificing more personal ends. Jung speaks of this when he writes:

> The right way, like the wrong way, must be paid for, and however much we may extol 'venerable

nature,' it is in any case an *opus contra naturam*. It goes against nature...not to yield to an ardent desire. And yet it is nature which prompts such an attitude in us...So it is as Pseudo-Democritus says: 'Nature rejoices in nature, nature conquers nature, nature rules over nature.' [Our] instincts are not all harmoniously arranged, but are perpetually jostling each other out of the way. The ancients were optimistic enough to see this struggle not as a chaotic muddle but as aspiring to some higher order...Whichever course one takes, nature will be mortified and must suffer, even to the death...Nobody who finds him[/her]self on the road to wholeness can escape that characteristic suspension which is the meaning of crucifixion. (Jung, 1966, pp. 261-262)

In Figure 3 (Chapter Three) I equated or paralleled gravity with "holy spirit." But if the latter is the power of the most subtle patterning, now identified with the higher forms of love, nothing really different is being said. With both of these aspects of gravity in the cosmos, we have what one of my friends has termed the "hologram of love."

FREEDOM

Freedom follows next because it makes possible choice and therefore consciousness. Actions arrived at unconsciously cannot be matters of conscious choice, but there must be options available before choice is possible. Teilhard stresses that the primordial "stuff of the universe" must be composed of "elementary freedoms," for "no other substance than this could produce the human molecule." (See Chapter Five.) Freedom is basically related to the number of options in a pattern, along with the energy available to pursue the options, that is, the applicability of "will" to the situation. These three elements can be traced in the evolutionary development of the cosmos.

Hydrogen atoms have a "repertoire" of several hundred basic patterns under conditions found in the cosmos, but the majority of these patterns are high-energy states which are unavailable to most H-atoms. An electron in a high-energy state can move to any lower-energy state, but by fairly strictly determined stages. At times a branching of the paths is possible, but the probabilities of one or the other being taken are determined and constant. This would indicate a lack of will. Nonetheless, even at this most primitive stage, the very existence of a branched path is symbolic of freedom. Among the paths from high-energy to low-energy states are also some that are taken very infrequently, called by physicists "forbidden transitions." By most of the rules for the changes in quantum numbers as the electron goes from state to state, the electron could *not* make such a leap, but in some cases it *does*. The fact that there are occasional exceptions to normal paths is also symbolic of freedom.

In radioactive decay of heavy nuclei, we also find choices of paths possible, again with definite probabilities as to which will be taken. Here an additional complication appears, for the nucleus can in some cases move from a higher energy state to a lower energy state by means of an intermediate state which has higher energy than either the starting or ending state.

If we picture Figure 8 as the cross section of a volcano-shaped sculpture with a ball in the central

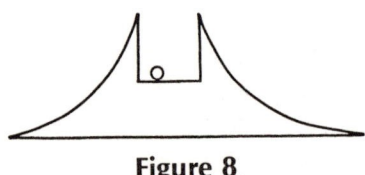

Figure 8

hole, it is clear that the ball could roll downhill to the surrounding ground if there were a path. But to get to the outside of the hole, the ball would need to be lifted to the top of the inner wall. It could not roll up this wall without violating the law of the conservation of energy. But again, the analogous process happens in the nucleus by means of a so-called "virtual state," in which the conservation of energy is "momentarily" violated.

The momentary excursion of energy is so brief that, according to the uncertainty principle, it cannot be detected. And when the particle is freed from the nucleus, it has just the amount of energy it would have if it had tunnelled out the inner wall on the level and rolled down the remaining hill. Here is another symbol of freedom (to violate physical laws momentarily) and a certain inwardness. It is like the minor embezzler who momentarily robs the petty-cash box to bet on a horse. If the horse wins, he repays the money before it is discovered and pockets the difference (the energy which the ball has as it rolls down the final slope). If the money is gone too long, the loss is discovered.

According to the uncertainty principle, the freedom is in the margin of error. The same kind of momentary violations of conservation of energy are actually responsible for the ability of nuclear particles to stick to each other.[3] This, in turn, makes

---

3. For example, a deuteron, or heavy-hydrogen nucleus, consists of a proton and a neutron. They stick together by grabbing particles of intermediate mass, called *mesons* from each other. While the meson is traveling between the proton and neutron, we have three particles, which momentarily violate the conservation of energy. Again, we say it is a "virtual" meson which is exchanged, and it can never be detected in flight between the proton and the neutron.

possible the complexification of hydrogen into the full range of chemical elements. Two such particles, say a proton and a neutron in a nucleus, "exchange" a "virtual" particle so quickly that the momentary deficiency of the one and the excess of the other cannot be detected. Prior to its discovery, the mass of the exchanged particle was predicted by means of the uncertainty principle as the maximum which could escape detection.

Another example of freedom on the atomic level is the ability of fundamental particles to assume either of the two disguises, wave or particle. For instance, it is said that a photon travels as a wave but interacts as a particle. As often noted earlier, the two aspects are mutually exclusive and logically contradictory, but both describe the *same* entity at appropriate times. Both are necessary to a complete description. Again we can see this as a branching process or element of choice, however primitive, on the part of the photon, electron, or other elementary entity. This wave-particle duality, as Heisenberg says (Chapter Four), leads to the uncertainty principle, where it limits our knowledge of complementary aspects of the state of an entity. Here, the physicist is forced to choose, to exercise freedom, as to which of the two aspects to measure. The "elementary freedom" (the entity) retains its freedom precisely in the irreducible margin of error by which the knowledge of its state is withheld from the physicist.

One possible way in which the error yields freedom in complexification is perhaps in the precise angles at which hydrogen atoms attach themselves to oxygen atoms to form water (Figure 9). The lines of centers of the atoms form an angle of 105°, whereas the perfect angle for the formation of a hexagram is 120°. This difference probably contributes greatly to the variability of snowflake patterns and thus yields freedom in its form as variety.

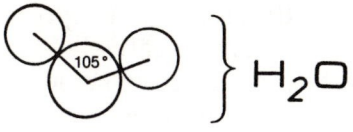

Figure 9

Jung defines will as "disposable energy" and says that the realm of psyche is that in which will is manifest (Jung, 1969c, pp. 181-184 and 200). The atom which takes one of two paths to a lower energy state does dispose of energy. It sends its energy outward and "relaxes" to a more compact, more stable state. We would hardly say that it exercises choice as to which path to take, but it *does* have the freedom to take one or the other. Freedom is prior to choice. At this level, freedom follows a relatively simple pattern in its alternatives.

Several points emerge. The symbol of disposable energy is present at the atomic level. The centration even of an atom releases energy to the environment. Also, it may well be that our psychic energy comes from a form of centration, just as a star's radiant energy comes first from gravitational centration, then from nuclear centration. Another point is that the available paths for the disposition of energy follow patterns which are quite definite on the atomic level but more complex later in evolution. The patterns within which human behavior normally occurs have been called *archetypes* by Jung.[4] Let us consider these points together.

---

4. Choiceful behavior must reckon with these patterns, but can modify their effects.

Physicists say that when the atom makes a transition from a high-energy state to a lower one, the electrons of the atom become more tightly "bound" to it. The electrical attraction of the positively charged nucleus pulls at each negatively charged electron and, if any attractive force is acted upon, energy is released. In order to produce energy for release, the electron must move closer to the nucleus. If it is as close as it can get (by the laws of quantum mechanics), it cannot release energy and it cannot, on its own, move to a higher energy state. That requires energy from outside. This outside energy is usually supplied by collisions with other particles. When that happens, energy may be transferred to the atom in question, and it then has disposable energy. This also means that in the collision it has become less tightly bound.

When a water molecule is about to bind onto an existing snowflake by freezing, it also goes to a lower state, gives up energy, and enters greater stability through being bound to the crystal. Here the pattern is much more subtle and the paths available much more numerous, but the process is still guided by a pattern. In principle, it is similar to the way in which electrons bind to atoms, but the bonds are more delicate and the repertoire correspondingly greater.

In psychic processes, analogies abound, though the processes must be much more complex because the interconnections are much more subtle. It is well-known that certain "complexes" or subpersonalities can be very loosely bound in a person's psyche and can split off and become autonomous. In normal persons the phenomena of learning exhibit an analogy to the binding of electrons to atoms. When the "aha" occurs in learning, it is as if something has fallen into place, and new energy is released. It often seems also as if the thing learned has been hovering around, just out of reach, waiting for an adjustment in the patterns of thought which would allow it a place of connection.

The interactions of humans in pairs, groups, and cultures show patterns in many ways, some quite simple and some extremely complex. To discuss these in detail would take us far afield indeed. When the normal patterns are broken—creatively or uncreatively—it seems that extraordinary energy has gotten into the situation. Such activity generally brings the collective pressures to bear with great weight, showing that normal patterns are strong indeed. Behavior which is merely rebellious rather than creatively different indicates one kind of freedom, but one much more collectively determined. Only a few in history have been real bringers of culture shifts, and it usually cost them their lives. Still, the fact that they have brought creative change also indicates that human energy was building to an excess which could move to a new level.

On a more personal level, often when we feel we are being extremely individual, we are actually being quite collective. Nowhere is this more evident than in the process of "falling in love." To an outsider, one's behavior is quite predictable, but the feeling of individuality and choice is remarkable. Still, we too are capable of sustained will in an *opus contra naturam*, and those who achieve creativity in their personal lives, whether famous or obscure, are the real heroes and heroines of evolution. They are the growing edge.

CONSCIOUSNESS

We are concerned here, not with the development of spirit and matter as such, but with the development of their meeting point, the psyche. Consciousness is a function of psyche. Spirit and matter are dual modes of our perception of reality. From what we can discern of the primordial stuff, hydrogen atoms, the spirit and matter aspects of this stuff are inseparable. Consciousness, however, *has* separated them so that they seem distinct and contradictory as modes of experience. Our ego-consciousness also tends to favor one or the other as primary. In the previous chapter, this view was shown to be untenable: there is no matter without spirit and no spirit without matter. It is now our task to realize their unity consciously, to participate in both, and thus to participate in the building of psyche, the field of consciousness.

The absolute prerequisite for ego-consciousness is the individual. It is always consciousness of particulars, of this or of that. Finitude is stressed in this situation. The whole field of things one *might* be conscious of is never fully present to one—only parts or aspects. Even a general sense of being, or of, say, goodness in the cosmos, is only a part. There are all the details, including detailed memories, which come to awareness sequentially. Individuals are finite.

It may help to contrast ego-consciousness—particularity consciousness—with omniscience. The physical symbol of omniscience is the overall patterning itself as it moves "matter" into organization at the simpler levels of evolution. The patterning of a snowflake evolves with the flake itself, as pointed out earlier. The subtle forces which move freezing water molecules into position do not arise *outside* the flake as if some *independent* consciousness were *designing* a flake. The potentials for all possible snowflake images are in the primordial hydrogen patterns.

Perhaps we may speak of these atomic patterns as designed, and perhaps not. They are, however, known to follow from certain combinations of small whole numbers (the "quantum numbers") and from general properties of space and time. The latter properties are conditioned by the relationships of matter in the cosmos, that is, by the entire cosmos and the distribution of matter within it. Wherever *design* seems to reside, it seems to be an area in which our intellects, as developed so far, are unused to function. We cannot yet penetrate this mystery.[5] In this area we again run into the "receding first cause." It is best, perhaps, to begin with the primordial stuff as given, which is patterned in the fashion described. Again we recognize that we begin in the middle.

To return to the description of omniscience, it is important to reiterate that the pattern and its complexity evolve from *within*, though ultimately conditioned from without. The snowflake probably must be said to be *unaware* of the image of itself which it generates. Yet somehow it "knows" how to fulfill its pattern in actuality. This unconscious (in the sense of ego-consciousness) knowing is what may be termed a fragment of omniscience. The total omniscience would then be the sum of such interacting patterns in the cosmos.

Reflexive consciousness (awareness, particularity consciousness) requires complexity. The primitive patterned forms of spirit-matter simply do not have sufficient complexity to have consciousness attributed to them. The brain is the only known organ capable of this awareness. Part of this capability depends on a highly developed perceptual system and part on analytical (intellectual) functions. Here

---

5. My wife says, "except perhaps for Mozart."

the evolutionary picture is most complete, and we see the gradations in the emergence over the aeons. At the same time we see the evolution of language, first emotive and later conceptual, and realize the continuity of the human with the near subhuman forms. This is especially evident in the limited but present capability for abstract concepts in chimpanzees.

These functions reside in *individuals*. Where herd or flock instincts or perceptions predominate, there is no real creativity or individuality, no consciousness. The behavioral patterns, however complex, are simply transmitted from generation to generation. The greatest individuals bring creative change and, even if they are killed by the old pattern in the process, the new has taken root. These are the most individual members of the species, the most differentiated from the group. As a psychoanalyst[6] said to me, "The hallmark of consciousness is creativity." This is not a function of perpetuated patterns, even though for example, the variety of snowflakes may symbolize creativity and individuality to us. Nothing a snowflake does might truly be called behavior.

The ultimate primitive symbol of the individual is the very finitude of our closed cosmos.[7] Next comes the existence of individual stars rather than a smooth uniform gas as our cosmos. The primordial gas broke into pieces because gravity separates as well as unites. The cosmos conforms to the image of the sphere whose center is everywhere and whose circumference is nowhere. The condition of being

6. Dr. Sheila Moon, who also authored the quotation which begins Chapter Two.

7. Though the question of whether the cosmos is finite and closed or infinite and open is still undecided, I am here risking a bet that it will be found to be closed.

omnicentered makes possible the individual, through breaking the stuff of the universe into hunks.

As the cosmos is multicentered, so also is proto-plasm, which does not uniformly cover or coat the earth with a smooth centerless mass. Rather, individuals complexify in the evolution of the species. Genetic excursions which become replicated are of great importance, along with the selection of sexual partners. Finally, the brain-in-the-body achieves sufficient complexity for consciousness to become possible.

As the organ becomes more complex, the internal interconnections become more subtle. This was previously brought out in the section on freedom. We do not merely have separation—differentiation into individuals—but internal differentiation as well: that is, specialized functions of organs, resulting in a web of internal interactions. As these become more numerous and delicate, what had been highly determined patterns of behavior move closer to freedom. It is practically the same thing to say that spirit can now express more of the potentials of the total patterning, or that spirit is now able to move matter more easily. A complexity is developing, not only of organic form and pattern, but also of the essential primordial link between spirit and matter: psyche. Here we must recall what has been said of freedom and will. Jung says:

> What I call the psyche proper extends to all functions which can be brought under the influence of a will...Psyche is essentially conflict between blind instinct and will (freedom of choice) (Jung, 1969c, p. 183).

And, as noted earlier, will or freedom follows from the production of excess energy, with multiple paths available. In order to make things clearer, we must use hindsight, knowing that consciousness has indeed emerged. Here the discussion of "reality" in Chapter Two assumes great weight: *all* of our knowledge and images are psychic in nature. We know that we do not perceive the thing-in-itself, whether it be matter or spirit. The existence of psyche needs no proof, but rather the existence of matter and spirit do.

> Matter and spirit both appear in the psychic realm as distinctive qualities of conscious contents. The ultimate nature of both is transcendental, that is, irrepresentable, since the psyche and its contents are the only reality which is given to us *without a medium.* (Jung, 1969c, p. 216)

Matter and spirit have been sufficiently well defined as aspects of reality.

Let us recall the diagram presented in Chapter Two:

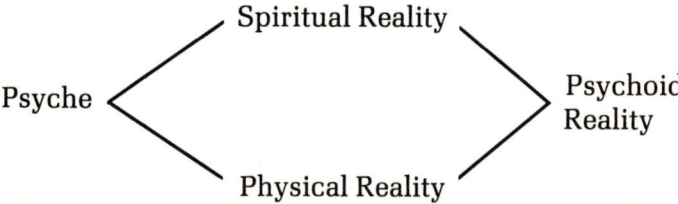

We began with the psyche and then classified the transpsychic realities behind our images and experience as spiritual reality and physical reality. Beyond that, in the ultimate *discernible* nature of things, spirit and matter must be seen as two aspects of a single unitary reality which Jung described as psychoid or archetypal. We have now seen that they have never really been separated except in our perception. As long as nature follows the patterns instinctively, the internal and interactive forces having dominance, there is no separation of spirit and matter. There is also, and precisely so, no consciousness, no will, no freedom.

Still, psyche is developing. The meeting point of spirit and matter is being complexified to the point of becoming capable of will or of freedom. One could also say that the inherent complexities in the patterning are being actualized because organic forms are more subtle and responsive to the patterning or spirit; the connections are more flexible. As consciousness grows and more of our life-patterns become amenable to will, we certainly may, following Jung's definition, speak of *building* the psyche. The field of choice is emergent as the balance and conflict of spirit and matter. We have our instinctual side which must be honored and our spiritual side which calls for the denial of instinct. The material forces are now sufficiently weak that a "new" opposition is revealed, that of the primordial duality of spirit and matter. Spiritualization is now strong enough to predominate over instincts in many cases, for ill or good. Read again the words of Jung quoted on pages 158-159. To those, we now add:

> For anyone acquainted with religious phenomenology it is an open secret that although physical and spiritual passion are deadly enemies, they are nevertheless brothers-in-arms, for which reason it often needs the merest touch to convert the one into the other. Both are real, and together they form a pair of opposites, which is one of the most fruitful sources of psychic energy. There is no point in deriving one from the other in order to give primacy to one of them. Even if we know only one at first, and do not notice the other until much later, that does not prove that the other was not there all the time. (Jung, 1969c, p. 212)

When spiritualized energy becomes as strong as

the instinctual, the field of choice is really open for the first time. But consciousness is more than choice. It also involves the representation or reflection of images, ideas, and emotions to a subject who somehow stands apart from them. There is a certain detachment of psyche from both matter and spirit, as if the interaction of spirit and matter has, or has now, a semi-independent existence.

The separating aspect of gravity has been mentioned in relation to the production of stars (based on the omnicenteredness of the cosmos), and so also the separation of protoplasm into evolving species and individuals. The development of sense organs which widen the field of perception immeasurably is of extreme importance, for the individual then stands "over against" not only the immediate environment but also the whole world, and even the entire cosmos. But even the reception of nerve impulses representing signals from without is not yet the reflection which is the awareness of self, and therefore the germ of ego-consciousness.[8] And ego-consciousness itself is not yet awareness of the deep-rootedness of consciousness in the unconscious psyche, which alone makes us at last aware of our collective assumptions and hidden motives. When this happens, we experience real freedom, choice, and individuality.

Self-reflexivity or ego-consciousness is thus a natural consequence of the physical separation of individuals from the rest of the world. Sense organs and brain complexity are also required so that we have sensory confirmation of the fact of separation

---

8. In a sense, the world leads the ego out of the unconscious. Senses elaborate themselves as responses to stimuli, and brain develops in response to that.

and the capacity to realize it. But the differentiation which leads to creative individuality is differentiation with respect to our psychic unconscious. We are so sustained from the unconscious that very few of us even perceive the fact. Only through differentiation from the unconscious can creative relationship to it occur.

The two major differentiations—the outer one from the world and from the tribe, and the inner one from the psychic unconscious—have been often symbolized as births. In this image the separation is clear, but also a new level of being self-sustained. We can, of course, never be self-sustaining in the sense of outward independence from all living forms. The same is true of our ultimate need for an inner life. To dream is a well-known but very elementary example of this need. But "self-sustained" can describe an independence from *local* happenings and vicissitudes, and therefore a deeper dependence upon totality. This is equivalent to the raising of the level of consciousness to include the depth dimension of reality, seeing more and more subtle aspects of the patterning. And that certainly may be described as a higher spirituality.

MEANING

Separation from our outer and inner worlds has been necessary in order for relationship to both worlds to occur. But we have not generally taken up these relationships with "will power." We have become cut off from, have lost contact with, the inner mythic dimension of our unconscious. We have forfeited awareness of its support, and therefore we experience meaninglessness.

Another way of expressing the idea of the mythic dimension of the unconscious is in terms of the internal reflections or images of the patterning. Myths are statements of the pattern for a culture.[9] Of course, many of the motif-patterns are common human patterns, present in the myths of all cultures. Contacts with these patterns, or events which parallel the patterns, generally are experienced as meaningful.

Consider a child successfully putting a square block into a square hole and learning shapes. Along with the learning, the success yields a feeling of having fulfilled an *intentionality*. These two go together. The same statement describes the phenomenon of "falling in love." There is a sense of a deeper intentionality in the moment, no matter what happens to the couple later.[10]

The child first seeks intention-fulfillment confirmation from parents and parent substitutes, later from institutions and society. Then, perhaps, an attempt is made to take all sense of worth *inside*. It is possible for an unreflecting person to spend many years in any of these states. At some point it will be necessary, if the individual is so "called," to seek out perception of a greater Patterning or will. To do this, as mentioned in the previous section, is to base one's

---

9. This is why it is futile for a modern individual to consciously attempt to write a myth.

10. That all unions do not "work out" is an indication that greater depth is required for relationship. It is important to note here, and I am especially indebted to Dr. Elizabeth Boyden Howes for pointing this out, that in such cases spirit and matter certainly do get together, but the meeting point (psyche) is not necessarily built up very much in the process. The pattern moves the individuals involved very powerfully indeed, but the *love* is not really substantial. It has no real solidity in the psyche. It is as if the two are united from below, from the primordial unity of spirit and matter, and not at the level of consciousness in the psyche. Such unions should perhaps be seen as temporary com-

being-in-the-cosmos on the widest possible scope. The acknowledgment of an ultimate dependence, since it is the truth, yields the greatest creativity and individuality precisely because it is one's deepest relationship. It puts responsibility on the individual for the perception of intentionality, something no institution (including a church or religious group) or other individual (including a guru or other spiritual guide) can do.

Meaning emerges through the appropriateness of perceived connections, through the sense of participation in the total Patterning, and through the energy which flows via the new connection. We say that it "clicks" together. In physics, the situation which produces or allows energy flow is called a resonance.[11] When we experience things which are numinous, we feel the energy flow in. Here, "numinous" is not limited to the conventional "religious" sense of the word. All energy inflow carries some kind of numinosity.

A word of caution is needed here: appropriateness emphatically does not mean comfort, though it does not exclude it either. It often means painful testing, not in the sense of a prescribed course of action or suffering, but by means of taking life as it really is.

---

pletions, for they are too powerful to be complex. The breakups which ensue often do much more for the building of consciousness than does falling in love. The painful moments in which caring is found, or else discovered to be nonexistent, play a large part in bringing forth new depths of personality. For much fuller accounts of relationship, the reader is referred to such books as *Human Relationship* by Eleanor Bertine (1958) and *The Inner World of Choice* by Frances Wickes (1963).

11. An example is tuning a radio. Many stations send out energy, but only the energy to which the radio is tuned is admitted and flows through the system to be amplified.

That we may dance or find humor at the moments of tragedy often shows the depth of the human spirit far more than growing old in dignity and apparent wisdom. We need to reflect upon what really moves us as greatness in others. Perhaps it is most often how people come through trials with increased humanity.

In evolution, then, we are looking for examples of appropriate connections. These include facts about the primordial stuff which Freeman Dyson (1979, p. 250-251) calls "numerical accidents." One of these is that the exact strength of nuclear forces must be as it is in the cosmos for life to develop. Other meaningful "accidents" enable water to exist as a liquid and carbon atoms to be the basis of life-molecules. Citing others as well, he says:

> I conclude from the existence of these accidents of physics and astronomy that the universe is an unexpectedly hospitable place for living creatures to make their home in.

Facts such as these, and they are numerous, reinforce our sense of intentionality in the pattern.

Random connection of the components of our DNA molecules could not have built the DNA strand to the minimum length—1500 units—for reproductive activity. The time required for random connections to do this is many orders of magnitude too great (Golay, 1961). Yet the connections did occur.

If, however, we think not of random connections but of connections guided by a pattern of potentials holographically, an additional pattern of forces is available for making *meaningful* connections. Another term for holographic evolution might simply be "pattern manifestation."

To bring together what has been said so far in this section, meaning-experiences occur when that which is guided holographically by the pattern actually occurs and, further, is grasped by conscious beings. Even when we grasp events of the past evolution, or see appropriate connection in the nature of spirit-matter, the meaning of creation is increased for us.

For us, who have been born in a time when human consciousness is split off from its support in the unconscious, this connection is often reconnection. *Reconnection* is the root meaning of *religion*, though that word has come to stand for a set of beliefs and/or practices and as such denotes a collective phenomenon. This is the case with all of the world's great religions, however much the individual benefits from adherence to these beliefs and practices. These benefits undoubtedly flow from the attitude of the individual, regardless of which religion (in the above sense) provides the containing framework. As Jung says:

> It is not ethical principles, however lofty, or creeds, however orthodox, that lay the foundations for the freedom and autonomy of the individual, but simply and solely the empirical awareness, the incontrovertible experience of an intensely personal, reciprocal relationship between [the hu]man and an extramundane authority which acts as a counterpoise to the 'world' and its 'reason.' (Jung, 1964a, p. 258)

Creeds and general principles are necessarily collective, but if the individual is of value, we must then look beyond collective forms to try to discern what religion may mean to a person. If individuals are cut off from their roots, *reconnection* with those roots will bring individuals religious experience.

The theology of Paul Tillich makes much use of this definition of religion. In his sermon, "You Are Accepted," and also in his books, *The Courage To Be* and *Biblical Religion and the Search for Ultimate Reality* (1964), he describes the separation as sin, as well as describing the basic belonging which brings "grace." This isn't the same as "I'm OK, you're OK," for we are and remain separated. Only thus can we be individual, and the knowledge which is available to us is not so easy to come by as Kierkegaard indicated when he stated both that innocence is ignorance and that the loss of innocence and ignorance is attained only by incurring guilt. "You are accepted," Tillich says, "accepted by that which is greater than you," and the courage to be is the courage to accept *being accepted* in spite of our separation and our unacceptability.

As Jung has demonstrated, the total human must include both the conscious and unconscious sides. What he calls the Self is the archetype of human totality, including the complementary opposites of conscious ◄⊖► unconscious, masculine ◄⊖► feminine, good ◄⊖► evil, and others. The Self is not only the archetype of human totality, but also the God-image within. To reconnect without ground also means to reconnect with the image of intentionality which brings meaning. What we experience as most deeply moving, profound, and meaningful conveys a sense of in-place-ness, or appropriate connection. I am suggesting that this is a complexified form of the sort of appropriateness of a water molecule finding its place in a snowflake, or even of a hydrogen atom finding its place in a water molecule. These are all actualizations of the patterning at their respective levels.

The patterning in its aspect as spirit, with its beyondness, its ability to organize visible forms in spirit-matter, its omniscience, and its tendency to produce consciousness and meaning through love and freedom, may well be described by the word *God*. The aspect of God which we call *person* has also been included in the tendency to produce individuals. We can even visualize this God as "word," as we perceive nascent meaning in reality and attempt to articulate it. The fact that God is perceived in the mythic dimension as one who speaks points to *word* as an aspect of the primordial "stuff-of-the-universe." The first chapter of Genesis repeats the phrase "and God said," and one of the principal Navajo deities is "Talking God."

To the above attributes of God, traceable in the holographic evolution of spirit-matter, must be added the attribute of continual newness. We have seen the ability of the holographic patterning to give birth to that which is new. The pattern always has more to "say" than can be actualized in any concrete form. This is why the new is continually emergent in evolution. The mythic God-image of the Divine Child corresponds to the continual birthing of the new and previously unforeseen in the plan of God. The Ancient of Days is also the Eternally New, in manifestation.

The opposites, spirit and matter, have occupied much of the book and yet at this point they become central again. The Self—human totality and God-image—joins spirit and matter just as effectively as it does the other pairs.

Values always partakè of both spirit and matter. This crossconnection between the two forces us to be creative, because spirit and matter are in continual conflict. If gravity complexifies to and operates as love, then moral qualities may be expected to be complexified aspects of spirit-matter. Then good and evil, because they both exist, would be seen as potentials of that spirit-matter. If separation complexifies to sin (Tillich), the same would be true. This is clear simply as a fact. Good and evil have evolved in the cosmos. We don't describe the killing done by animals as evil but as a part of the greater pattern. But there is evidence that chimpanzees begin to feel, and other animals exhibit or can be taught to exhibit, shame-behavior.

Human totality and the God-image within are both complexes of opposites. This fact holds tremendous implications for our freedom and responsibility. Humanity is too young to have had more than glimmerings of these implications. We have tried to see God in various one-sided ways: only light and not also dark; only outside and not also inside; only spirit and not also matter. But God's image and law have been written into the "stuff of the universe" from the beginning of physical creation. Physical stuff *is* spirit-matter. The opposites, spirit and matter, *are* reconciled in the primordial stuff. Again, it is our conscious side which has split them apart in our thought and attitude.

The images of hydrogen atoms which were given in Chapter Five are closely related to images which have been central symbols in all religions and cultures. Circles with crosses, i.e., mandalas, have been God-images for millenia untold. We also speak of God's design in nature. In the atoms are images of hearts, brains, animal forms, and much more. These are the *primordial* forms, and for this reason, as well as the others, they are in fact God-images. Not only visual forms, but our experiences of freedom, meaning, love, and awe in our interactions with the rest of the cosmos, are also complexified forms of potentials which are already inherent in spirit-matter. Teilhard de Chardin called these atoms "elementary freedoms" and noted that only out of elementary freedoms, and not out of elementary determinisms, could humanity evolve. We have seen that the prototype of freedom is there in the atom itself, in that its nature embodies the uncertainty principle and for other reasons. The forms of our bodies with their organs, our human capabilities, our "coinherence" (see below) in a unified organic cosmos, and the mandala or God-image within us, are all written upon the heart of spirit-matter.

If this is so, as I feel it is, we can look to mythical material and certain other kinds of spontaneous writings for messages from the Patterning. For instance, in the book of Jeremiah, we read:

> But this is the covenant which I will make with the house of Israel after those days, says the LORD: I will put my law within them, and I will write it upon their hearts; and I will be their God, and they shall be my people. And no longer shall each [one] teach his[/her] brother, saying, 'Know the lord,' for they shall all know me, from the least of them to the greatest, says the LORD. (31: 33-34)

Here is a prophecy! Surely we feel that this is something to be desired, but from what we see we might be inclined to say that it certainly hasn't happened yet. People do not act the way we imagine they would act if God's law were in fact written upon their hearts. I say, very carefully, "the way *we imagine* they would act." But how can we know how people *would* act? And what about *us*? Do we feel that we act from the law written upon the heart? Or, do we in some other way *know* the inward law of God? Perhaps it is possible that we know but fail to act, or even that we act from the inward law without knowing it because of our preconceptions as to what that law really is. How can we discover this law?

The prophecy directs us to look inward. God says,

"I will put my law *within;* upon the heart." How deeply within are we to look? My answer: all the way to the very nature of our physical existence, to the stuff out of which we are made. The law is written upon the heart of matter. But let us begin nearer to where we live. I have three key terms for the exploration of the within: organism, freedom, and the balance of opposites.

What clue does organism hold for the "law written upon the heart"? And how can *we* be more organic and whole? Organism seems to be one major aspect of the "within of things."[12] It is also linked to freedom because we are most free when we are most at one with ourselves and act from our whole selves. In a sense, this is the most *natural* way to be, but it is also the most difficult thing to do. We could do it easily if we remained as unconscious as animals. Our conscious side, however, tends to cut off parts of ourselves—particularly the darker aspects, but also the greater ones—and to give them no honor in our lives. When we are angry at others, it is usually because their behavior corresponds to some part of ourselves which we cannot face. They are doing what we would do if we *let* ourselves do it. Our present human consciousness actually fears to know its own humanity. That is why it prefers the cosmos as bits rather than as organism. Increased consciousness, however, will not be a return to an unbroken primal unity, but a regathering of the very pieces which it has played such a strong role in scattering. We can work to recognize the places where we have split off our darknesses and greater potentials alike, projecting them onto others as villains or heroes.

---

12. Teilhard uses this expression in *The Phenomenon of Man* (1961), Chapter 2.

The first suggestion as to the law written upon the heart is, then, that of achieving a wholeness or organism of the personality. This organism must make the fullest use of our rational or separative powers, but not be caught in them, unable to face the fact of our irrational, dark, and unknown parts. In addition, we tend to value completion of a pattern and fail to honor the breaking up of completed patterns, which leads to new life. Thus we build walls of protection about all which seems to be working for us, fail to explore the "unimaginable possibilities for good" (Phillips, et al, 1975, p. 257) in our potentials, and prefer to keep them unknown. Wholeness requires that our unknown parts be brought into relationship with consciousness—even those parts split off by means of guilt or abhorrence.

If the law of God is not mere obedience to rules but the reconciliation of opposites for the sake of the organism which humanity is, freedom to suspend rules for the sake of reconciliation is implied. It may be that our very freedom manifests the presence of the Divine within. That God is freedom is not a new thought, but how many of us have considered the possibility that *our freedom* may be God's law within, written upon the heart? Perhaps our freedom is more in the realm of imagination and less in action. If it remains so, then we avoid the task which is presented at every moment.

We have not been educated to freedom and cannot learn it without making horrible errors. It is painful to live in times when the old bonds are breaking. But if we can no longer find all the behavioral or role models *outside,* we—all of us who are struggling to find consciousness—are then forced to find the law of God written upon the heart. God said, "I *will* write it." It *is* written, but that very law is a law of freedom, of nonconstraint, demanding a painful learning through trial and error. As Teller says, the means of reconciling opposites is "by no means obvious." *Inherently* so. Still, it has a clear goal: the reconciliation of the freedom of the individual with the rest of humanity. Charles Williams, British essayist and novelist, gave us some potent images in connection with his concept of "coinherence." We live by "mutual derivation" from each other. Williams said, "We may or may not live *for* each other, but whether we like it or not, we do live *from* each other." (Shideler, 1962, p. 48) Our dependence on each other, obvious as it is, is often difficult to accept because of our pride and notions of self-reliance. We often hate to accept what others, nature, and God give us. Williams said:

> Hostility begins to exist...when we think that we can choose by whom we will be nourished...If the web of humanity is in any sense one...then we precisely must live from, and be nourished by, those whom we most wholly dislike and disapprove. (Williams, 1958, p. 113)

This does not mean that we must not challenge or fight against that which we dislike. Numerous current situations in the world involving torture and repression require our concern and action. But even those who, like Hitler, show us the most extreme evil and degradation of which humanity and therefore we are capable, nourish us with this knowledge. We are sobered and we grow in consciousness and wisdom, provided we accept the nourishment. Then we can see our coinherence in the web of humanity and we know the awful range of our freedom. When we are able to reconcile the fact of good and evil in the world, then we also are able to recognize that we must reconcile the good and evil in ourselves to find life. And when we work to accept and transform the evil in ourselves, reconciling it with the good, we can more clearly perceive real outer evils. What we do not learn to recognize inwardly is thrust outside, "projected" onto others where it is lived out as an evil fate. Since it is the power inherent in the patterning which does this, we may fairly call such a fate the "wrath of God."

Frances Wickes quotes the following dream of a woman:

> I am on my way to the temple of music. I see before me the gleaming white columns that lead to the portal. But just in front of me is a pile of dirt that covers the narrow path from edge to edge. I draw back, looking for a way around it so that my white garment will not be soiled. A voice says, "Why do you draw aside? It is out of this dirt that the stars are made." (Wickes, 1963, p. 55)

This is a clear message not only that darkness must be faced, but also that it may be transformed. It even implies that transformed darkness is the source of light. It may be that we have no other light.

The love of God and the wrath of God are in the Pattern of God. In the Jewish midrash tradition, God prays, "May it be my Will that my love overcome my wrath." If we can help the love overcome the wrath, we are going with the Patterning most creatively. Entering the Patterning to change it can be either creative or uncreative. We are now cocreators for good or ill. Causing the death of species changes the pattern, as does causing, say, the development of disease-resistant plants or insecticide-resistant predators. Genetic engineering can certainly change the emergent. Computerization as a human phenomenon, and the harnessing of various forms of energy also changes our focus of will and therefore what will emerge. Most of these developments have not occurred in a very wide choice field, that is, one based upon cosmic concerns. In general, we have seen only the possible benefits and have not let consciousness of the dangers bring us into conflict with ourselves.

Conflict forces us to be creative, to choose for higher rather than lower values if we will. Whatever our patterned development has empowered us to do is, or can be, part of what was desired from the beginning, whether creative or uncreative. If we hold, with the Latin poet Terence, that nothing human is alien to us, we see the awesome scope of our responsibility.

We can influence the pattern; our choices, in other words, affect God. As one author has said, "The uniqueness of [our] tiny fragment of the eternal affects the total eternal uniquely (Howes, 1971, pp. 88-89).

The indications are that choice as to the outcome of the human moral dilemmas for our world has been given over by God into the substance. Einstein said that he refused to believe that God plays at dice with the universe. Now it seems that He/She does so with much deeper risk than Einstein even conceived of. Einstein limited his consideration to the path by which an atom will go to a lower energy state. If the midrash prayer of God is a true message, the consequences of this choice are to help establish the very Will of God.

The only possible way to participate creatively in this process is to practice developing our perception of the trend of the emergence of the Patterning in both its spiritual and material aspects. There is much we can perceive about the nature of both, even from everyday experience, *with applied consciousness added.*

Only now that humanity has achieved such separateness as at present has it become possible to begin to take a creative relationship to the rest of the cosmos. We are first separated, but then we can *know* the cosmos, can know ourselves, can know each other, can know God. As part of evolution, the ego or the I appears as a reflection of that from which it is separated: it says "I am," which is the name God gives for Her/Himself to Moses. This separated I of ours seems therefore to be here for a *purpose.* That a fulfilled individual creativity and relatedness to the whole are part of that purpose seems to me evident from the facts which we have been considering. The relatedness through knowing is what I have been stressing. The word *individual,* though, implies uniqueness, creativity, newness, eternal variations on the basic human pattern. What we can know are our own roots and this knowledge, whether in the fields of science, religion, or psychology, is religious in the best definition of that word: it re-establishes a link with something from which we are separated.

We can *know,* but what do we mean by that? Our knowledge is never ultimate, as our consciousness is never ultimate, or we would be destroyed as individuals. "Who can see God, and live?" as it was said in the Hebrew Scripture. We attempt to *describe* as a means of knowing. Mathematics is quite good as a language in the physical sciences, but in the end it is only a way of putting things and other ways are needed as well. What we know is embodied in our descriptions of the nature of things: of matter, spirit, and psyche. These descriptions always miss the mark because we remain separated, but to a reasonable degree they also hit the mark because we share the nature of these things.

Because there is a unity at a higher level behind the opposites which we experience at the level of our ego-consciousness, both opposites are always necessary for a relatively complete knowing. As Kierkegaard said, "Existence is contradiction," and we should not be surprised to find contradictory descriptions of spirit, and even of God, because contradiction is necessary in the description of matter, as in the case of waves and particles in physics. It is my deep conviction that the created universe must reflect the nature of the Creator.

If science studies matter and religion studies spirit, which is also a way of putting it, and these two—matter and spirit—are related as I have described, then it is obvious that knowledge gained from both is necessary for a complete description of reality. They seem to oppose each other at crucial points, but we must learn to live in that tension, for each tension calls upon us to be creative. And again, creativity is only possible because of separation, i.e., because of our individuality and finiteness. The necessity of both of the mutually exclusive approaches does not and cannot yield the *resolution* of the contradictions inherent in the two approaches; rather, it can help to fit the contradictions into the universal pattern of the separation and unity of opposites. Creativity to reconcile them in ourselves is also required.

If science studies matter and religion studies spirit, and together they provide a glimpse of a complete view of reality, then what does each seek as its object of knowledge? Bronowski (1966, p. 36) said that science seeks truth, but what it finds is knowledge. The parallel statement would be that religion seeks the good[13] but must also remain content with something less ideal, for which I have used the word *appropriate*. We remain separated from the truth and the good which we seek, and yet ultimately we belong to them. And as we seek them, somehow they are brought into actuality, as value realized. Because we are separated, we continue to seek; we are *involved*, and what we do in the clarification and actualization of good and truth assumes extreme importance. The way in which we as individuals reconcile the opposites of spirit and matter is "by no means obvious." This is a field of choice for us, and choice is the means of personal growth.

The convergence of religion and science, then, is not a total merging of the two, though the spirit-matter that they study is much more of a unity than previously imagined. The convergence is a fitting of both methods into a unity which describes a person's relationship to the universe, so that the two reflect each other in depth. I can't say all that I can see as ramifications of that last sentence, but at a *minimum* I see the complexification of spirit-matter as the ground of a new consciousness of God which is just emerging, and I share with Teilhard a vision of this field of consciousness as a new ground of God's becoming.

---

13. In *Descent Into Hell* (1949, p. 16), Charles Williams has a naive character say, "Nature's so terribly good. Don't you think so?" And the protagonist says, "Yes...but when I say *terribly* I think I mean *full of terror*. A dreadful goodness." It is in this sense that I mean *good*. It may ultimately be the case that truth cannot be distinguished from goodness, but we commonly imagine things which are true but not good, and vice versa.

Appendix A
Particles and Waves

The two criteria by means of which we may distinguish the concepts of "particle" and "wave" are *divisibility* and what I will call boxability, both of which are expressions of a question of continuity. The first of these is an internal consideration, and the other relates to the environment of a putative particle. A particle is indivisible and boxable; a wave is divisible and unboxable. Thus, in each, one quality is affirmed and the other is denied.

To further amplify these criteria, something is boxable only if it can truly be said that all of it can be contained inside a box. It is then definitely discontinuous from what is outside. If we put an object into a box—if we specify an area of confinement—but cannot be certain that it is entirely within, we would say that it is not boxable; it is not a "nice neat" particle. In the everyday world we can fulfill the boxability criterion for a great many objects.

An object is *divisible* if it can be divided indefinitely without losing its identity. An object which cannot be so divided is, in fact, discontinuous and is not a wave. A particle of water (H_2O), for instance, can be divided into two particles of hydrogen and one particle of oxygen, but it then ceases to be water; it loses its identity. A single molecule of water is indivisible *as water* because it becomes something else. Divisibility means the possibility of infinite subdivision *without* loss of identity. Therefore we must be certain that we can identify an object being tested. If a particle of energy in the form of blue light were

191

divided into two particles of half the original energy, it would become red light particles.

In these examples, the fact that a particle is boxable and indivisible has been illustrated.

It is a bit more difficult to see that a wave is divisible, but cannot be boxed. A wave is usually drawn as follows:

This may be pictured as the surface of water seen cross-sectionally, as in an aquarium, or it may be abstractly envisioned as a graph of some quantity which varies regularly in time or space. If it is a light wave it will be moving, carrying a flow of energy, and will vary in time at a given point in space, or in space as viewed at a given instant.

The wave is drawn with dotted lines at the ends to indicate that the mathematical expressions by which one may quantify this behavior (attach a measure-number to it) extend indefinitely in either direction. The basic characteristics of waves are their "wavelength," "amplitude," and spatial velocity. Of these, the wavelength will enter into the discussions to follow. This is the distance between two wave "crests," measured in meters or other suitable units. Its symbol is l.

amplitude

The amplitude of a wave is pictorialized as half of the vertical distance between "crest" and "trough." For light, it measures the strength of the electric and magnetic fields involved in appropriate units. All light waves move at a constant velocity of approximately 300,000 kilometers per second in a vacuum.

If a wave is not regular, as below,

it is always seen as the net effect of many superimposed *regular* waves, each with a single *pure* wavelength and amplitude. The amplitudes, or the *effects* of these waves at a given point, are simply added to or subtracted from each other. For example, pictorially adding the two waves on the left:

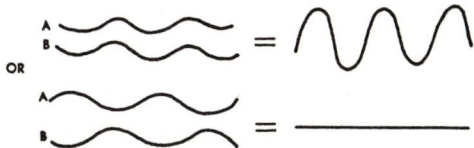

If the basic identity of a wave is given by its wavelength, we can picture a given wave as the sum of many waves with much smaller amplitude, but all with the same wavelength and all lined up crest-to-crest. Thus a wave is divisible without loss of identity. For any given irregular wave, it is possible to analyze its "components" in this way.

The case of a "boxable wave" is instructive, for it shows up the contradiction inherent in that notion. What we want is this:

To the left of A, and to the right of B, there is to be no disturbance, and between A and B there is to be a pure wave. Lines are drawn extending in both directions from the "active" interval, for to describe the wave *in* the interval we must still use components which extend indefinitely beyond it, but we specify that their effects cancel each other *everywhere* outside the interval. Therefore, in any case, our consideration extends indefinitely in space. This is one reason why such a wave is not boxable. Moreover, and we will return to this point later in this section, though the wave appears to be *pure* (of a single wavelength) in the interval, the components *must* be of many wavelengths. The greater the accuracy demanded for the "fit" of the description to the given wave, the more wavelengths are needed. Thus even a wave which *appears* to conform to the diagram cannot be identified because it really has no purity of wavelength. A pure wave cannot be boxed.

There is an experiment in which the central component is a pair of holes. If light consists of particles, each particle logically must proceed through one or the other but not *both* of the holes. The light going through the apparatus was adjusted so that *if* the light consisted of particles, they would be going through one at a time. This experiment, as mentioned earlier, may also be performed with electrons, which ordinarily are thought of as particles, so it is not hard to imagine them going through one at a time.

After passing the two holes (or through one of them, as the case may be), the light forms a pattern on a screen or on a photographic plate. If the light goes through both holes, the pattern is radically different from the pattern formed if the light goes through only one hole at a time. We just look at the pattern to see whether the light goes through one or two holes.

Now in the experiment, the pattern formed was *always* the two-hole pattern, so whatever went through—wave or particle—went through both. But since a particle cannot go through both, that theory was excluded. After this experiment, physicists thought that they had proved that light was wavelike.

However, another experiment, based on Einstein's 1905 explanation of the ability of light to transfer its energy to electrons, was done a few years later and proved that this phenomenon cannot be explained in terms of a wavelike nature of light but *only* by the particle theory.

Appendix B
The Uncertainty Principle

The uncertainty principle, in its most common form, states the theoretical impossibility of simultaneously measuring both the position and the momentum of a particle to any arbitrary degree of precision. That is, it *specifies* the maximum accuracy obtainable. One can measure either one to an accuracy which is not theoretically limited, but each increase in the precision of the knowledge of one entails a loss of precision in the knowledge of the other. It is generally agreed that precise knowledge of *both* is prerequisite to a complete specification of the "state" of the particle. The uncertainty principle is the *quantitative* aspect of complementarity. Heisenberg, quoted by Cropper in *The Quantum Physicists*, says:

> "[Bohr] took objection to the fact that I had not started from the dualism between particles and waves." But the two physicists resumed their work with discussions "which were not devoid of stress," and soon it was evident "that the uncertainty relations were just a special case of the more general complementarity principle." (Cropper, 1970, p. 122)

We will accept this point of view in all that follows: namely, that the uncertainty principle falls within complementarity as the quantitative aspect of the latter, and that, as a special case of complementarity, it represents complementarity wherever it (the uncertainty principle) is found to hold true.

Naturally, one must consider the need for measuring these particular quantities simultaneously, or even at all. We must ask whether or not there are other possible descriptive systems, i.e., systems employing *other* fundamental concepts. However, the quantities which are subject to the uncertainty principle are precisely the ones which are the subjects of our most fundamental *notions* (space and time) and laws (the conservation of energy and momentum).

Appendix C
Kierkegaard on the Concept of Time

"When time is correctly defined as infinite succession, it seems plausible to define it also as the present, the past and the future. However, this distinction is incorrect, if one means by it that this is implied in time itself; for it first emerges with the relation of time to eternity and the reflection of eternity in it. If in the infinite succession of time one could in fact find a foothold, i.e., a present, which would serve as a dividing point, then this division would be quite correct. But precisely because every moment, like the sum of the moments, is a process (a going by), no moment is a present, and in the same sense there is neither past, present, nor future. If one thinks it possible to maintain this division, it is because we *spatialize* a moment, but thereby the infinite succession is brought to a standstill...On the other hand, so soon as we let one moment succeed the other we posit the present.

"The present, however, is not the concept of time, unless precisely as something infinitely void, which again is precisely the infinite vanishing...

"On the contrary, the eternal is the present. For thought, the eternal is the present as an annulled succession (time was succession, going by). For visual representation, eternity is a going-forth, yet it never budges from the spot, because for visual representation it is a present infinitely rich in content. Likewise in the eternal there is not to be found any division of the past and the future, because the present is posited as the annulled succession.

"So time is infinite succession. The life which is in time and is merely that of time has no present. It is true that to characterize the sensuous life it is commonly said that it is 'in the instant' and only in the instant. The instant is here understood as something abstracted from the eternal, and if this is to be accounted the present, it is a parody of it. The present is the eternal or rather the eternal is the present and the present is full." (Kierkegaard, 1957, pp. 76-78)

References

Abbott, Edwin. 1952. *Flatland*. New York: Dover.

Adler, Gerhard. 1974. Basic concepts of analytical psychology: Guild Lecture No. 174. London: *The Guild for Pastoral Psychology*.

Auden, W.H. 1969. For the time being. *Collected longer poems*. New York: Random House.

Bentley, W.A., and Humphreys, W.J. 1962. *Snow crystals*, New York: Dover.

Bertine, Eleanor. 1958. *Human relationship*. New York: David McKay.

Blake, William. 1975. *The marriage of Heaven and Hell*. London: Oxford University Press.

Bohr, Niels. 1934. *Atomic theory and the description of nature*. Cambridge: Cambridge University Press.

———. 1963. *Essays 1958-1962 on atomic physics and human knowledge*. New York: Random House, Vintage Books.

Bronowski, J. 1966. *The identity of man*. New York: Doubleday, Natural History Press.

Cropper, William H. 1970. *The quantum physicists and an introduction to their physics*. New York: Oxford University Press.

d'Espagnat, Bernard. 1979. Quantum theory and reality. *Scientific American*. 241:16, 158-60 + (Nov.).

Dyson, Freeman. 1979. *Disturbing the universe*. New York: Harper and Row, Colophon Books.

Einstein, Albert, 1949. Autobiographical Notes. In *Albert Einstein: philosopher-scientist*. Edited by Paul A. Schilpp. LaSalle, IL: Open Court.

———. 1935. *The world as I see it*. Translated by Alan Harris. New York: Covici-Friede.

Feynman, Richard P. 1966. The development of the space-time view of quantum electrodynamics. *Science:* 153, 699-708.

———. 1963. *Lectures on physics, volume I*. Edited by Robert B. Leighton and Matthew Sands. Reading, MA: Addison- Wesley.

Freedman, D. Z., and P. von Nieuwenhuizen. 1978. Supergravity and the unification of the laws of physics. *Scientific American*. 238:16, 126+ (Feb.).

Golay, Marcel. 1961. Confessions of a communications engineer. *Analytical Chemistry*. 33: 23A-31A.

Heisenberg, Werner. 1971. *Physics and beyond*. New York: Harper and Row.

Hitchcock, John L. 1976. *A comparison of 'complementarity' in quantum physics with analogous structures in Kierkegaard's philosophical writings, from a Jungian point of view*. Dissertation 76-9150. Ann Arbor: Xerox University Microfilms.

Holton, Gerald. 1973. *Thematic origins of scientific thought: Kepler to Einstein*. Cambridge, MA: Harvard University Press.

Howes, Elizabeth B. 1971. *Intersection and beyond*. San Francisco: The Guild for Psychological Studies.

Jaffe, Aniela. 1971. *From the life and work of C. G. Jung*. Translated by R. F. C. Hull. New York: Harper and Row.

———. 1970. *The myth of meaning*. Translated by R. F. C. Hull. London: Hodder and Stoughton.

Jammer, Max. 1966. *The conceptual development of quantum mechanics*. New York: McGraw-Hill.

Jantsch, Erich. 1980. *The self-organizing universe*. New York: Pergamon.

Jung, C. G. *Collected works,* Bollingen Series XX. Translated by R. F. C. Hull. Princeton: Princeton University Press.

_____. 1959. *Aion. Collected works* 9ii.

_____. 1969a. *The archetypes and the collective unconscious. Collected works* 9i.

_____. 1964a. *Civilization in transition. Collected works* 10.

_____. 1964b. With Marie-Louise von Franz, Joseph L. Henderson, Jolande Jacobi, and Aniela Jaffe. *Man and his symbols.* Edited by C. G. Jung. New York: Doubleday.

_____. 1963. *Memories, dreams, reflections.* Compiled and edited by Aniela Jaffe. New York: Random House.

_____. 1966. *The practice of psychotherapy. Collected works* 16.

_____. 1969b. *Psychology and religion: West and East. Collected works* 11.

_____. 1969c. *The structure and dynamics of the psyche. Collected works* 8.

_____. 1956. *Symbols of transformation. Collected works* 5.

Kant, Immanuel. 1965. *Critique of pure reason.* Translated and edited by Norman Kemp Smith. New York: St. Martin.

Kierkegaard, Soren. 1957. *The concept of dread.* Translated by Walter Lowrie. Princeton: Princeton University Press.

_____. 1962. *Philosophical fragments.* Translated by David F. Swensen and Howard V. Hong. Princeton: Princeton University Press.

_____. 1954. *The sickness unto death.* Translated by Walter Lowrie. Princeton: Princeton University Press.

Kuhn, Thomas S. 1970. *The structure of scientific revolutions.* Chicago: University of Chicago Press.

Lauer, Quentin. 1965. *Phenomenology.* New York: Harper and Row, Harper Torchbooks.

Lenzen, Victor F. 1949. Einstein's theory of knowledge. In *Albert Einstein: philosopher-scientist*. Edited by Paul A. Schilpp. LaSalle, IL: Open Court.

Mascaro, Juan. 1962. *The bhagavad gita*. Baltimore: Penguin Books.

Moon, Shiela. 1970. *A magic dwells*. Middletown, CN: Wesleyan University Press.

Nagel, Ernest, and James R. Newman. 1958. *Gödel's proof*. New York: New York University Press.

Neumann, Erich. 1954. *The origins and history of consciousness*. Translated by R. F. C. Hull. New York: Pantheon.

Otto, Rudolf. 1958. *The idea of the holy*. Translated by John W. Harvey. New York: Oxford University Press, Galaxy.

Phillips, et al. 1975. *The choice is always ours*. Wheaton, IL: Theosophical Publishing House.

Polanyi, Michael. 1962. *Personal knowledge*. New York: Harper and Row, Harper Torchbooks.

Popper, K. R. 1967. Quantum mechanics without "the observer." In *Quantum theory and reality*. Edited by Mario Bunge. New York: Springer-Verlag.

Scheibe, Erhard. 1973. *The logical analysis of quantum mechanics*. New York: Pergamon.

Schwarzschild, Martin. 1958. *The structure and evolution of the stars*. Princeton: Princeton University Press.

Shideler, Mary M. 1962. *The theology of romantic love*. New York: Harper and Brothers.

Sinnott, Edmund. 1955. *The biology of the spirit*. New York: Viking.

Taylor, Edwin, and John A. Wheeler. 1966. *Spacetime physics*. San Francisco: W. H. Freeman.

Teilhard de Chardin, Pierre. 1969. *Human energy*. Translated by T. M. Cohen. New York: Harcourt Brace Jovanovich.

_____. 1961. *The phenomenon of man*. Translated by Bernard Wade. New York: Harper and Row, Harper Torchbooks.

Teller, Edward. 1969. Niels Bohr and the idea of complementarity. In *Great men of physics*. Edited by Marvin Chachere. Los Angeles: Tinnon Brown.

Tillich, Paul. 1964. *Biblical religion and the search for ultimate reality*. Chicago: University of Chicago Press, Phoenix Books.

_____. 1948. *The shaking of the foundations*. New York: Charles Scribner's Sons.

von Franz, Marie-Louise. 1974 *Number and time*. Evanston, IL: Northwestern University Press.

_____. 1966. *Puer aeternus*. New York: Spring Publications.

Weisskopf, Victor F. 1979. *Knowledge and wonder*. Cambridge MA: The MIT Press.

Wheeler, John Archibald. 1962. *Geometrodynamics*. New York: Academic Press.

White, Harvey E. 1931. Pictorial representations of the electron cloud for hydrogen-like atoms. *Physical Review* 37:1416-1434.

Whitehead, Alfred North. 1969. *Process and reality*. New York: Macmillan, Free Press.

Wickes, Frances. 1963. *The inner world of choice*. New York: Harper and Row.

Williams, Charles. 1958. *The image of the city*. London: Oxford University Press.

Index

a priori/a posteriori, 60,
74-76, 81-83, 87
Abbott, Edwin, 126, 128n,
199
actuality, 47-49, 127
Adler, Gerhard, 101, 199
Agazziz, Louis, 113
apperception, 72, 74
appropriate connections,
175-178
archetypes/archetypal, 50,
53, 83-84, 89, 107, 119,
163, 170
Aristotle, 60
atoms, 21, 154, 163, 180.
See also hydrogen
Auden, Wystan Hugh, 94,
199

being/existence, 30, 46-54;
ground of being, 50
Bell, John S., 117n
Bentley, W.A., and
Humphreys, W.J., 143,
199
Bertine, Eleanor, 175n,
199

Blake, William, 118, 199
Boehme, Jacob, 73, 199
bonds, 154-156, 164-165;
chemical, 139; nuclear,
155
brain, 22, 23, 46, 123,
145-148
Bronowski, Jacob, 188, 189

carbon, 155
cause, causality, 100,
111-112
centration, 84, 88, 153,
158, 163
choice/choose/choosing,
159, 163, 172, 186, 189
complementarity, 17, 24,
93, 94-117, 126, 195;
formal characteristics
of, 100, 101
complexification/complex-
ified/complexity, 16,
78-85, 89, 142-146, 152,
179, 189; ladder of,
154-156
compounds, chemical, 142,
155

concepts/conceptual, 42,
77-81, 84, 89, 100, 103,
120, 124, 196
consciousness, 4, 12-28,
34, 67, 72, 78, 87, 110,
123, 153, 159, 165-173,
177, 182; human (ego-
consciousness), 22, 64,
108-113, 119, 166, 172
constants of nature,
132-136
continuity/discontinuity, 7,
18, 20, 97; connection/
disconnection, 67
contradiction, 6, 9, 95, 98,
162, 188; hard/soft, 17,
97-103, 109. See also
opposites
cosmos, 11, 16, 19, 85-90,
141, 149, 152, 157, 158,
160, 167, 181
Cropper, William H., 195,
199

d'Espagnat, Bernard, 117,
199
Descartes, Rene, 60
description, 42, 95, 97,
100, 120, 122, 124, 188;
See also phyics, laws of
dimensions/dimensional-
ity, 126, 131, 133; num-
ber of, 126-128
discontinuity. See
continuity
Divine Child. See newness
DNA molecules, 72n,
155-156, 176
duality, wave-particle, 20,

97-98, 103, 124, 140, 162,
191-194; experimental
basis of, 97, 191-194, 195
dynamism, 100, 107,
112-113, 157
Dyson, Freeman, J., 176,
199

ego, or 'I', 58-59, 68-73;
I/not-I polarity, 32,
36-37, 67, 73
ego consciousness. See
consciousness, human
Einstein, Albert, 18, 32,
52, 57, 63-65, 74, 76, 92,
105, 122, 123, 141, 186,
194, 200
electron, 20, 97, 139, 154,
160
elementary freedoms, 15,
42, 85
elements, chemical, 6, 51,
141, 152. See also
individual elements
Eliot, Thomas Stearns, 40
emergence/emergent, 111,
168. See also newness
energy, 82, 85, 87-89, 116,
124, 154-156, 159, 161,
163-165, 175
entelechy, 148-149. See
also purposiveness
entities, fundamental, 18,
30; number of, 131-136
evil, 33, 184. See also
values
evolution, 5, 15, 21, 44-45,
77-78, 82-83, 89, 122,
145-146, 151-189

existence, 31, 71;
properties of, 51, 127.
See also being/existence

fact, 3, 7, 19, 62, 94, 96,
120, 124; guiding, 5, 18,
44, 96, 122, 124
Feynman, Richard P., 8,
40, 97, 200
forbidden transitions, 160
forces, physical, 129-131,
152
Freedman, D.Z., and P.
von Nieuwenhuizen,
130, 200
freedom, 159-165, 169, 179,
183. *See also* elementary
freedoms

Genesis, book of, 179
gluons. *See* quarks
God/God image, 3, 10, 12,
16, 22, 24, 28, 43, 46, 65,
148, 149, 178-181, 183,
185-189; God-circle, 66,
85, 90, 168
Godel, Kurt, 61, 95, 96,
124
Golay, Marcel, 176, 200
good. *See* values
gravity, 89-90, 128, 130,
152-154, 157, 179

healing, 119, 145, 158
Heisenberg, Werner, 8, 92,
105, 195, 200
helium, 141

Henyey, Louis G., 40
Hitchcock, John L., 18,
100, 200
holography/hologram, 22,
146, 159, 179
Holton, Gerald, 1, 101,
107, 200
holy spirit, 86, 90
Howes, Elizabeth, Boyden,
174, 186, 200
human/humanity, 23, 149,
153, 180, 182, 184,
186-187
Hume, David, 31
Husserl, Edmund, 58, 60,
61
hydrogen, 21, 22, 137-142,
154, 160, 166, 178, 180

image, 14, 31, 38, 71-72,
77, 84, 89, 93, 119-120,
124, 139, 148, 166, 180
indeterminacy. *See*
uncertainty principle
individuals, 153, 158, 165,
166, 168-169, 173, 177,
187
instinct. *See* spirit-instinct
polarity

Jaffe, Aniela, 36, 45, 88n,
200
Jammer, Max, 97-106, 200
Jantsch, Erich, 5, 200
Jeremiah, book of, 181
Jesus of Nazareth, 151
Jung, Carl Gustav, 9, 24,
31, 34, 42, 61-62, 68-70,

77-78, 101n, 108, 111, 117, 156, 158, 163, 171, 177, 201

Kant, Immanuel, 32, 39, 42, 47, 60, 61, 73-76, 79-80, 201
Kierkegaard, Soren, 9, 47-49, 52, 102, 128, 178, 188, 197, 201
knowledge/knowing, 1, 9, 11, 12, 13, 19, 28, 31, 63, 65, 83, 92-93, 114, 122, 167, 187, 188; opposed to belief, 114
Kuhn, Thomas, S., 1, 200

ladder of complexification. *See* complexification
language, 77-81, 84, 103, 139, 187
Lauer, Quentin, 61, 200
Lawrence, Brother, 73
Lenzen, Victor, 74, 202
life-molecules, 142
light, 20, 97, 124, 133. *See also* photon
love, 151-153, 157, 178, 179

Mach, Ernst, 150
mandala. *See* quaternity
mathematics, 11, 19, 61, 83, 85, 94, 95, 117, 123, 124, 133, 137, 140, 187
matter, 8, 12, 14, 15, 44, 90, 93, 123, 128, 140-152,

188; and antimatter, 52, 53, 89; properties of, 30, 51, 75-76. *See also* spirit-matter
meaning, 9, 70, 87-89, 173-177; and learning, 72-73
middle, being in the, 11, 30, 150
models, physical, 18
Moon, Sheila, 29, 168, 202
morality, 183-187. *See also* choice
Mozart, Wolfgang Amadeus, 167
myth/mythic dimension of the psyche, 173-174

Nagel, Ernest, 79, 202
necessity, philosophical, 31, 49, 61
Neumann, Erich, 67, 68, 107, 202
newness, emergent, 179
Newton, Sir Isaac, 57, 65, 123, 131
not-I. *See* ego
nuclei, atomic, 153-155, 160
number, 118-120, 126-136, 144-146, 155, 167. *See also* forces, entities, dimensions
numinous/numinosity, 24, 84, 85, 175

object/objective/objectiv-ity, 12, 32, 112-113, 122

observer/observation, 64, 100, 105-106, 123-124

Occam's razor, 56

omniscience (contrasted to ego-consciousness), 23, 166-167

opposites, 28, 43, 95, 113-117, 119, 121, 180; relatedness of, 6, 17, 23; as mutually exclusive, 17, 94; needed for completeness, 17. See also contradiction, hard/soft

Otto, Rudolph, 24, 202

pair production. See antimatter

Parmenides, 66

particle. See duality, wave-particle

patterns/Patterning, 5, 28, 42, 53, 81-82, 89, 118, 123, 137, 140, 142, 146, 156, 165, 174-175, 178, 181, 185

perception/perceive, 42, 44, 72, 74, 82, 121; nonperceptual background, see unus mundus

phenomenon/phenomenology/phenomenological grounding, 30, 54-62, 117

philosophy, 11, 60, 80, 94, 108, 114

photon, 51, 132, 139. See also light

physics/physical, 11, 15, 50, 71, 85, 94, 95-108, 129-136, 153, 160; laws/equations of, 41, 57, 64, 103, 137, 161

pine tree, 144-145

Plato, 66

Poincare, Henri, 113

Polanyi, Michael, 26, 202

Popper, Karl R., 81, 202

possibility, 49

projection/projected, 185

psyche/psychic, 23, 31, 34, 43, 64, 71, 111, 166, 169-171; "infra-red" and "ultra-violet", 45

psychoid, 42, 44, 45, 82, 170. See also reality

purpose/purposiveness, 3, 5, 88. See also entelechy

quarks and gluons, 50, 53

quaternity, 66, 87-90, 116, 117, 120

reality, 30-62; archetypal, 39, 43, 54; diagram, 58, 59; as limitation, 33, 34; physical, 36-38, 47, 54, 108, 111; as psychic, 34; psychoid, 43, 46, 54; spiritual, 38-46, 47, 54, 108; ultimate, 43, 46, 47, 54

relativity, theory of, 52, 116, 123, 141

religion, 2, 27, 177, 187; and science. See science and religion

Rhine, J.B., 47
Rig Veda, 63. See also
  Mascaro, Juan

Sagan, Carl, 156
Scheibe, Erhard, 11, 19,
  63, 202
Schrodinger, Erwin, 141
Schwarzschild, Martin, 39,
  64, 76, 202
science and religion,
  convergence of, 12, 93,
  188-189
Scriven, Michael, 78
Self, 10, 65, 90, 109,
  148-149, 178
separation/separated/sepa-
  rateness, 12, 27, 92, 122,
  152, 179-180, 187-188
Shideler, Mary
  McDermott, 184, 202
Sinnott, Edmund, 144, 202
snowflakes, 21, 22, 142-144
space, 126-127; and time,
  116, 127-128
spirit-matter, 15, 64,
  118-150, 166, 170-171,
  179-180, 189
spirit/spiritual, 12, 14, 15,
  21, 39-42, 44, 45, 86-90,
  93, 118, 123, 137, 148,
  156, 171, 188; spirit-
  instinct polarity, 45, 91,
  92, 171-172
stars/stellar, 16, 41, 46, 51,
  141, 152-154, 163
stuff of the universe, 20
subject/subjective/subjec-
  tivity, 12, 71

supergravity. See unified
  field theory
supernova, 154
synchronicity, 44

Talking God (Navajo
  deity), 179
Taylor, Edwin, 134, 202
Teilhard de Chardin,
  Pierre, 4, 14, 42, 48,
  84-85, 87, 120-121, 159,
  202
Teller, Edward, 17, 98-107,
  184, 203
temperature, 154-157
Terence, 186
theology, 11, 24, 94
thing-in-itself (Ding an
  Sich), 2, 30, 74
Thurman, Howard, 71
Tillich, Paul, 2, 27, 35, 71,
  92, 177, 180, 203
time, 127-128, 197-198. See
  also space and time

uncertainty principle, 8,
  123, 135, 139, 161,
  195-196
unconscious, the/that
  which is, 5, 18, 44, 95,
  108-113, 120
unified field theory,
  130-131
unity, 9, 31, 90n, 97, 100,
  119, 170, 189; fundamental, see unus mundus; as
  nonrational, 100,
  106-107, 111. See also
  opposites

universe. *See* cosmos
unus mundus, 43, 44
uranium, 141

values, 179, 188-189;
  good/evil, 95
virtual particles, 161n, 162
von Franz, Marie-Louise,
  14, 42, 108-109, 111, 120,
  128, 202
von Neumann, John, 104
von Nieuwenhuizen. *See*
  Freedman, D.Z.

wave. *See* duality, wave-
  particle
Weisskopf, Victor, 145,
Wheeler, John Archibald,
  129n, 133-135, 141n,
  157, 203

White, Harvey E., 42, 138,
  203
Whitehead, Alfred North,
  81, 95, 96, 203
whole/wholeness, 13;
  patterns of, 144-145. *See
  also* healing
Wickes, Frances, 175n,
  185, 203
will as disposable energy,
  12, 34, 82-83, 111-113,
  159, 163, 169-170
Williams, Charles, 184,
  189n, 203
within of things, the, 4
world, outer or external,
  31, 37, 54-55, 114

yin-yang symbolism,
  113-117

Readers of Quest books will be
interested in these titles—

Two Faces of Time—*By Lawrence W. Fagg*
A challenging, comparative study of time as it is understood by
science and religion.

The Theatre of the Mind—*By Henryk Skolimowski*
The eonic drama of our growth from instinct to mind, to the intuitive, and beyond. "Glory to evolution," concludes the author.

The Transcendent Unity of Religions—
By Frithjof Schuon
A study of the exoteric and esoteric aspects of religion

Available from:
The Theosophical Publishing House
306 West Geneva Road
Wheaton, Illinois 60189

21